Get more gr  !

click

search

print

cook

From apple pie to zucchini bread, we've got you covered. Browse our free online recipes for Guaranteed Great!™ results.

You can also sign up to receive our **FREE online newsletter**. You'll receive exclusive offers, FREE recipes & cooking tips, new title previews, and much more...all delivered to your in-box.

So don't delay, visit our website today!

www.companyscoming.com

visit our 🍴 website

Company's Coming Cookbooks

Quick & easy recipes; everyday ingredients!

Original Series

- Softcover, 160 pages
- Lay-flat plastic comb binding
- Full-colour photos
- Nutrition information

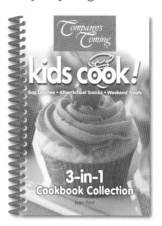

3-in-1 Cookbook Collection

- Softcover, 208 pages
- Lay-flat plastic coil binding
- Full-colour photos

Original Series

- Softcover, 160 pages
- Lay-flat plastic comb binding
- Full-colour photos
- Nutrition information

Special Occasion Series

- Softcover, 176 pages
- Full-colour photos
- Nutrition information

For a complete listing of our cookbooks, visit our website:
www.companyscoming.com

Table of Contents

The Basics of
Barbecuing

Appetizers

Burgers
& More

Entrees

Side Dishes

Condiments,
Rubs &
Marinades

The Company's Coming Story

Jean Paré (pronounced "jeen PAIR-ee") grew up understanding that the combination of family, friends and home cooking is the best recipe for a good life. From her mother, she learned to appreciate good cooking, while her father praised even her earliest attempts in the kitchen. When Jean left home, she took with her a love of cooking, many family recipes and an intriguing desire to read cookbooks as if they were novels!

"Never share a recipe you wouldn't use yourself."

When her four children had all reached school age, Jean volunteered to cater the 50th anniversary celebration of the Vermilion School of Agriculture, now Lakeland College, in Alberta, Canada. Working out of her home, Jean prepared a dinner for more than 1,000 people, launching a flourishing catering operation that continued for over 18 years. During that time, she had countless opportunities to test new ideas with immediate feedback—resulting in empty plates and contented customers! Whether preparing cocktail sandwiches for a house party or serving a hot meal for 1,500 people, Jean Paré earned a reputation for great food, courteous service and reasonable prices.

As requests for her recipes increased, Jean was often asked the question, "Why don't you write a cookbook?" Jean responded by teaming up with her son, Grant Lovig, in the fall of 1980 to form Company's Coming Publishing Limited. The publication of *150 Delicious Squares* on April 14, 1981 marked the debut of what would soon become one of the world's most popular cookbook series.

The company has grown since those early days when Jean worked from a spare bedroom in her home. Today, she continues to write recipes while working closely with the staff of the Recipe Factory, as the Company's Coming test kitchen is affectionately known.

There she fills the role of mentor, assisting with the development of recipes people most want to use for everyday cooking and easy entertaining. Every Company's Coming recipe is *kitchen-tested* before it is approved for publication.

Jean's daughter, Gail Lovig, is responsible for marketing and distribution, leading a team that includes sales personnel located in major cities across Canada. Company's Coming cookbooks are distributed in Canada, the United States, Australia and other world markets. Bestsellers many times over in English, Company's Coming cookbooks have also been published in French and Spanish.

Familiar and trusted in home kitchens around the world, Company's Coming cookbooks are offered in a variety of formats. Highly regarded as kitchen workbooks, the softcover Original Series, with its lay-flat plastic comb binding, is still a favourite among readers.

Jean Paré's approach to cooking has always called for *quick and easy recipes* using *everyday ingredients*. That view has served her well. The recipient of many awards, including the Queen Elizabeth Golden Jubilee Medal, Jean was appointed Member of the Order of Canada, her country's highest lifetime achievement honour.

Jean continues to gain new supporters by adhering to what she calls The Golden Rule of Cooking: *Never share a recipe you wouldn't use yourself.* It's an approach that has worked—*millions of times over!*

Foreword

Barbecuing has many virtues. It's a quick and easy way to cook almost any food, making it a perfect fit with our busy lives. It's the only method of cooking that gets us outdoors and lets us take advantage of warm weather. Barbecuing lets us relax and enjoy making food for family and friends. It's quite possibly the most fun cooking you'll ever do! And don't let the weather stop you—*Everyday Barbecuing* is your year-round resource for great grilling recipes!

To help you get the most from your barbecue, we've created this cookbook full of fabulous flavours and great grilling ideas. Our recipes cover appetizers to main courses to side dishes, and we've included both recipes that can be made in less than 30 minutes and recipes designed to feed a crowd. From simple and quick to extra special, we've got you covered—all you need to do is fire up the barbecue!

Whether you're looking for familiar fare or something with a bit more flair, look no further than *Everyday Barbecuing*. On the more traditional side, Grilled Potato Skins and Golden Beer Can Chicken are sure to please the gang and keep the backyard party hopping. If an elegant

dinner is more your style, try delicious Cranberry Salmon on Cedar and Grilled Corn Provençal—a feast for both the eyes and taste buds.

Our recipes cover not only a great range of ingredients, but also a variety of barbecuing methods. From quick steaks that take minutes to grill over direct heat, to slow-cooked roasts done over indirect heat using the rotisserie, you can experiment with various cooking techniques as you create delicious food. Cut down on cooking and cleanup time, and bump up the flavour with *Everyday Barbecuing*!

Jean Paré

Nutrition Information Guidelines

Each recipe is analyzed using the most current version of the Canadian Nutrient File from Health Canada, which is based on the United States Department of Agriculture (USDA) Nutrient Database.

- If more than one ingredient is listed (such as "butter or hard margarine"), or if a range is given (1 – 2 tsp., 5 – 10 mL), only the first ingredient or first amount is analyzed.
- For meat, poultry and fish, the serving size per person is based on the recommended 4 oz. (113 g) uncooked weight (without bone), which is 2 – 3 oz. (57 – 85 g) cooked weight (without bone)—approximately the size of a deck of playing cards.
- Milk used is 1% M.F. (milk fat), unless otherwise stated.

- Cooking oil used is canola oil, unless otherwise stated.
- Ingredients indicating "sprinkle," "optional," or "for garnish" are not included in the nutrition information.
- The fat in recipes and combination foods can vary greatly depending on the sources and types of fats used in each specific ingredient. For these reasons, the amount of saturated, monounsaturated and polyunsaturated fats may not add up to the total fat content.

Vera C. Mazurak, Ph.D.
Nutritionist

The Basics of Barbecuing

Simply defined, barbecuing is the act of cooking food over a charcoal or gas heat source. It's an ancient, elemental method of cooking that puts us in touch with our inner caveman! Its enduring popularity is largely because it's a quick, healthy and simple way to prepare food and entertain family and friends in the warm months of the year, when we all long to be outside enjoying the weather and having fun. For many people, summer and barbecuing just go together, while for some other brave souls, barbecuing is a year-round activity that no amount of bad weather can prevent!

While the tools and appliances that we use to barbecue have become more sophisticated over the years, the simple pleasure of cooking food outside over a heat source has remained essentially the same.

"Barbecuing" Versus "Grilling"

The terms "barbecuing" and "grilling" are often used interchangeably, and while they do overlap, they refer to different activities. Barbecuing refers to cooking done specifically on a barbecue appliance of some type; grilling is a broader term referring to food cooked on metal bars over any heat source, including barbecues, indoor grills and grill pans. Also, while barbecuing is mainly an outdoor activity, grilling can be done indoors or outdoors. The focus of *Everyday Barbecuing* is on barbecuing rather than grilling, and all the recipes in the book have been designed to be cooked on an outdoor barbecue.

Types of Barbecues

The range of barbecues available these days is much greater than it once was. The kind of barbecue you choose can be the result of various factors, such as how much you want to spend, how much space you have for storage, how often you barbecue and for how many people—and even your own personal opinions about cooking. Below is a brief look at some standard barbecue options.

CHARCOAL-FIRED BARBECUES

Of the two main types of barbecues, charcoal grills are the more traditional. They provide the "cooking over an open fire" experience that many people enjoy about barbecuing. The burning of charcoal also creates smoke, and for those who want to impart a distinctive smoky flavour to their food, charcoal grills are the best choice. Flavoured wood chips of various kinds, such as hickory and mesquite, can be added to burning charcoal to vary the flavour produced by the smoke.

Fans of grilling over charcoal think of it as an event that requires more ability and attention than cooking with gas. Building a good fire and controlling the heat require a little more skill than simply pressing a switch to light up a gas heating element, so a charcoal grill is probably a better choice for people serious about the activity of barbecuing itself, and not for those who mainly want to barbecue food quickly and conveniently.

An increasingly popular tool for starting charcoal fires is a sheet metal cylinder known as a chimney starter, which is positioned at the bottom of the barbecue and filled with charcoal briquettes. Crumpled newspaper is stuffed into the bottom of the cylinder and lit, and in 20 minutes or so, when the coals are covered with a grey ash, they are hot enough to cook over and can be dumped onto the fire grate. This tool makes it easier to start the barbecue, especially if you are not comfortable around, or experienced with, lighting fires.

Of all the styles of charcoal barbecues out there, the kettle grill is possibly the best known, and probably the most popular. With its domed shape, it's deep enough to double as an oven, making it great for both direct and indirect grilling.

GAS/PROPANE BARBECUES

This type of barbecue has become very popular over the last 20 years, probably due to the perceived advantages it has over the charcoal grill. Fuelled by either propane or natural gas, a gas barbecue doesn't create the same warm, glowing atmosphere as a grill that burns charcoal or wood, but it does offer many conveniences: it's easier to keep clean; doesn't produce smoke when lit (which may please your neighbours); is simpler and safer to ignite; heats up quickly; and offers easy, and sometimes very precise, temperature control. Also, many feel that a gas barbecue distributes heat better than a charcoal grill, giving better and more consistent cooking results. For a lot of people, a gas grill just makes barbecuing simple and easy, leaving them more time to enjoy the food and visit with family and friends.

For this book we have used a natural gas barbecue for all recipes, but a propane or charcoal-fired grill may be used with equally good results.

Standardized Temperatures

Whether you use gas or charcoal, please note that the recipes in Everyday Barbecuing use terms such as "Low," "Medium" and "High" instead of temperatures to indicate levels of heat. Refer to the following chart for the temperature rangeseach term represents. These ranges apply to both direct and indirect methods of cooking:

LOW	300°F – 350°F	(150°C – 175°C)
MEDIUM-LOW	350°F – 400°F	(175°C – 205°C)
MEDIUM	400°F – 450°F	(205°C – 230°C)
MEDIUM-HIGH	450°F – 500°F	(230°C – 260°C)
HIGH	500°F+	(260°C+)

If you have a barbecue with no temperature gauge, use an oven thermometer to make sure the temperature of your barbecue is in the correct range.

Barbecuing Methods

DIRECT HEAT

Direct heat is a high-heat method of grilling directly over a heat source, be it gas burners or hot coals. This method works best for food items that you want seared and caramelized on the outside, but still moist and juicy on the inside, for example, steaks, boneless chicken breasts, burgers and hot dogs. Direct heat is ideal for food that requires less than 25 minutes of cooking time.

INDIRECT HEAT

Indirect heat is a slow, low-heat method of cooking that mimics an indoor oven. The heat is turned on under one side of the barbecue while the food is placed on the other side instead of directly over the heat. Hot air circulates inside the grill to cook food from all sides for even cooking, similar to a convection oven. Indirect heat is best suited to large cuts of meat and foods that require cooking times longer than 25 minutes, such as a whole chicken or fish, ribs or large roasts, or delicate items that might burn over direct heat. For indirect heat to work properly, the barbecue lid must be kept down throughout the cooking process. If the lid is lifted, heat escapes and cooking time is longer.

Each recipe in *Everyday Barbecuing* provides directions for how to prepare a gas barbecue for direct and indirect cooking, and following our instructions will produce the best results. In our recipes, the barbecue lid is kept closed during all cooking, both direct and indirect. If you are using a charcoal grill, cooking with indirect heat will require you to set up a drip pan—a shallow aluminium foil roasting pan works well—in the centre of the fire grate and arrange hot coals around it. Place your food directly over the drip pan and close the lid.

ACCESSORIES

Some useful barbecuing accessories are listed below. We've included instructions for how to use them in our recipes.

Smoker Box: a small, perforated steel or cast iron container that holds wood chips. Used to provide a source of smoke for gas barbecues. To make your own smoker box, add soaked and drained wood chips to a 7 x 3 inch (18 x 7.5 cm) disposable

10

foil pan. Cover tightly with foil. Poke a few holes in the foil to allow smoke to escape.

Rotisserie: a spit, or long metal skewer, that suspends or rotates food, typically large cuts of meat, over a barbecue's heat source. Allows for even cooking that can be done mostly unattended.

Grill Basket: hinged wire container with long handles made to hold delicate foods that might otherwise stick to or fall through the grill of the barbecue, or be hard to turn, such as fish fillets, vegetables and tofu.

Beer Can Chicken Roaster: an inexpensive wire frame with a wide base made to hold a beer or soda can upright and stable while the chicken sits over it. Reduces the risk of the can tipping over during cooking.

Cedar Plank: a piece of untreated cedar made for barbecuing fillets of fish such as salmon. Should be soaked in warm water for several hours before being used on the grill to prevent warping, splitting and burning.

These are just a few of the many barbecuing accessories available. The more you use your barbecue, the more you may want to explore using other grilling tools.

Barbecue Safety Tips

- Always follow manufacturer's instructions for operating your barbecue, especially for the type of fuel required and how to start it up.

- Ensure that your barbecue is located on a level and stable site before lighting it up.

- Keep your barbecue in a safe spot sheltered from winds and flying debris.

- Keep your barbecue a safe distance from all flammable materials in the yard and garden.

- Once a barbecue is lit, do not move it.

- Keep children and pets away from a hot barbecue and make sure cooking is supervised by adults.

- Do not leave a hot barbecue unattended.

- Wear protective gloves when using any hot barbecue equipment such as tongs, grill baskets, smoker boxes, etc.

- If using a gas barbecue, make sure all sources of gas, such as valves and cylinders, are closed off once you're done grilling. Turn off all heat sources on the barbecue.

- Don't use flammable liquids or lighting fluids when barbecuing or you may cause a dangerous fire or explosion.

- Don't throw hot coals into plastic garbage bags or bins. Pour water on coals when finished and wait until they are cold to throw them out.

Food Safety Tips

When you do fire up the barbecue, make sure that food is prepared, cooked and served safely by taking the following precautions:

- Use only fresh meat, fish and poultry that have not been allowed to warm prior to cooking. At the grocery store, select these items last and check that the packaging is intact.

- Transport food in a cool environment, such as in an insulated cooler or in ice-packed bags, or in an air-conditioned car.

- Thaw frozen foods, particularly meat, fish and poultry, in the refrigerator and not on the kitchen counter.

- Wash hands thoroughly in hot, soapy water before handling any food.

- Prevent cross-contamination by keeping raw meat and its juices away from all other foods. Use a separate cutting board and knife to cut raw meat and cooked meat, and never place cooked meat on the same plate with raw meat or on a plate where raw meat has been sitting. Wash all cutting boards, plates, utensils, countertops and other areas that have come into contact with raw meat thoroughly with hot, soapy water to eliminate any bacteria. Ordinary dish soap will work fine; there is no need to use anti-bacterial cleaners.

- Cook ground meats thoroughly until no pink is visible, and the internal temperature specified by the recipe has been reached.

- Keep hot foods hot and cold foods cold. Never leave food out in the sun. Wait until you are ready to eat before serving and then set food out in shaded areas.

- Marinate foods in the refrigerator, not on the counter, unless directed to do so by a recipe. Generally it is safe to marinate vegetables at room temperature for short periods, but meat, fish or poultry should always be refrigerated. If you want to use leftover marinade to baste your food once it's grilling, first bring it to a rolling boil for at least five minutes to kill any bacteria.

- Don't judge the doneness of cuts of meat by their external colour because it can be deceiving. Use an instant-read thermometer, and always insert it into the thickest section of the meat to ensure that it is cooked thoroughly. Doneness temperatures are provided in all recipes in *Everyday Barbecuing*. Make sure the temperature you measure matches the one required by the recipe.

Now that we've covered all the basics, it's time to put on that apron, grab some tongs and fire up the grill. Happy barbecuing!

Roasted Red Pepper Hummus

The soft, nutty flavour of roasted garlic blends perfectly with caramelized onion and sweet peppers in this aromatic, flavourful dip. It's even better the second day when the flavours have had a chance to mellow.

Medium unpeeled onion	1	1
Small garlic bulb	1	1
Medium red peppers, halved	3	3
Can of chickpeas (garbanzo beans), rinsed and drained	19 oz.	540 mL
Lemon juice	2 tbsp.	30 mL
Olive (or cooking) oil	2 tbsp.	30 mL
Dried oregano	1 tsp.	5 mL
Ground cumin	1 tsp.	5 mL
Salt	1/4 tsp.	1 mL

Wrap onion loosely in greased foil. Trim 1/4 inch (6 mm) from garlic bulb to expose tops of cloves, leaving bulb intact. Wrap loosely in greased foil. Preheat barbecue to medium-high. Place packets on ungreased grill. Close lid. Cook for about 30 minutes, turning occasionally, until soft. Let stand until cool enough to handle. Remove and discard peel and stem-end from onion. Chop. Transfer to food processor. Squeeze garlic bulb to remove cloves from skin. Add cloves to food processor. Discard skin.

Place red peppers on greased grill. Close lid. Cook for about 15 minutes, turning occasionally, until skins are blistered and blackened. Transfer to large bowl. Cover with plastic wrap. Let stand for about 15 minutes until cool enough to handle. Remove and discard skins. Add peppers to food processor.

Add remaining 6 ingredients. Process until smooth. Makes about 3 1/2 cups (875 mL).

1/4 cup (60 mL): 64 Calories; 2.7 g Total Fat (1.6 g Mono, 0.6 g Poly, 0.3 g Sat); 0 mg Cholesterol; 9 g Carbohydrate; 2 g Fibre; 2 g Protein; 84 mg Sodium

Wrapped Cheese Packets

For a chic, upscale appetizer, try these bite-sized morsels of softened Camembert and toasted nuts. Unwrap the grape leaves and spread the melted cheese over crostini, baguette slices or even thin apple wedges.

Large grape leaves, rinsed and blotted dry, stems removed	8	8
Ginger (or orange) marmalade	4 tsp.	20 mL
Chopped walnuts, toasted (see Tip, page 86)	2 tbsp.	10 mL
Camembert cheese round, quartered	4 oz.	225 g

Arrange grape leaves on work surface. Spoon marmalade and walnuts in centre of 4 grape leaves.

Top each leaf with cheese. Bring up sides of leaves, folding over cheese on all sides to enclose. Invert packets onto remaining grape leaves. Bring up sides of leaves, folding over on all sides to enclose. Secure with wooden picks. Preheat barbecue to medium-high. Place packets, seam-side down, on greased grill (see Note). Close lid. Cook for about 3 minutes until leaves are browned. Turn. Cook for 1 minute. Transfer to individual serving plates. Remove and discard wooden picks. Makes 4 packets.

1 packet: 131 Calories; 9.5 g Total Fat (2.3 g Mono, 2.1 g Poly, 4.6 g Sat); 20 mg Cholesterol; 6 g Carbohydrate; trace Fibre; 7 g Protein; 471 mg Sodium

Note: Packets may be made 1 or 2 days ahead and grilled right before serving.

Kasbah Camembert

North African spices and creamy French cheese are great complements to crisp fruit slices or crackers. Lovely served with a well-chilled, semi-dry white wine.

Liquid honey	2 tbsp.	30 mL
Ground cumin	1 1/2 tsp.	7 mL
Ground cinnamon	1 tsp.	5 mL
Dried crushed chilies	1/2 tsp.	2 mL
Salt	1/4 tsp.	1 mL
Camembert (or Brie) cheese round	4 oz.	125 g

(continued on next page)

Appetizers

Combine first 5 ingredients in small cup.

Brush both sides of cheese with honey mixture until coated. Preheat barbecue to medium. Place cheese on greased grill. Close lid. Cook for about 3 minutes per side until softened. Serves 4.

1 serving: 125 Calories; 7.1 g Total Fat (2.0 g Mono, 0.2 g Poly, 4.3 g Sat); 20 mg Cholesterol; 10 g Carbohydrate; trace Fibre; 6 g Protein; 386 mg Sodium

Pictured on page 17.

Fiery Wings

Crispy grilled buffalo wings get an extra chili kick from sambal oelek, and make a lower-fat alternative to deep-fried wings. Starting with a spice rub adds great depth of flavour.

Cooking oil	2 tbsp.	30 mL
Chili powder	1 tsp.	5 mL
Coarse salt	1 tsp.	5 mL
Paprika	1 tsp.	5 mL
Pepper	1 tsp.	5 mL
Celery seed	1/2 tsp.	2 mL
Split chicken wings, tips discarded (or chicken drumettes)	2 lbs.	900 g
Butter (or hard margarine), melted	2 tbsp.	30 mL
Chili paste (sambal oelek)	2 tbsp.	30 mL
Louisiana hot sauce	2 tbsp.	30 mL

Combine first 6 ingredients in large bowl.

Add chicken wings. Toss until coated. Preheat barbecue to medium-low. Place wings on greased grill. Close lid. Cook for about 15 minutes per side until no longer pink inside.

Combine remaining 3 ingredients in small bowl. Brush over wings. Close lid. Cook for about 3 minutes per side until crisp and golden (see Note). Transfer to serving platter. Makes about 24 wing pieces (or 16 drumettes).

1 wing: 62 Calories; 4.0 g Total Fat (1.5 g Mono, 0.8 g Poly, 1.2 g Sat); 19 mg Cholesterol; trace Carbohydrate; trace Fibre; 6 g Protein; 184 mg Sodium

Note: If a barbecue flare-up occurs, move the wings to one side of the grill until flames die down. If you must, a light spritz from a water bottle can control small flames. Serious flare-ups should be doused with baking soda.

Grilled Potato Skins

Crispy and chewy, smoky and cheesy, potato skins done on the barbecue disappear fast. Sour cream makes a great accompanying dip.

Unpeeled medium baking potatoes	3	3
Cooking oil	2 tbsp.	30 mL
Chili powder	1 tsp.	5 mL
Ground coriander	1/2 tsp.	2 mL
Ground cumin	1/2 tsp.	2 mL
Salt	1/4 tsp.	1 mL
Pepper	1/4 tsp.	1 mL
Bacon slices, cooked crisp and crumbled	6	6
Grated Monterey Jack cheese	1/2 cup	125 mL
Grated sharp Cheddar cheese	1/2 cup	125 mL
Thinly sliced green onion	2 tbsp.	30 mL

Poke several holes randomly with fork into potatoes. Microwave, uncovered, on High for about 10 minutes, turning at halftime, until tender (see Tip, page 134). Wrap in tea towel. Let stand for 5 minutes. Unwrap. Let stand for about 5 minutes until cool enough to handle. Cut potatoes lengthwise into quarters. Scoop out pulp, leaving 1/4 inch (6 mm) shells. Save pulp for another use.

Combine next 6 ingredients in small cup. Brush over both sides of shells. Preheat barbecue to medium. Place shells, skin-side up, on greased grill. Close lid. Cook for 5 minutes. Turn over. Close lid.

Sprinkle remaining 4 ingredients over top. Close lid. Cook for about 3 minutes until cheese is melted. Makes 12 potato skins.

1 potato skin: 93 Calories; 6.6 g Total Fat (2.4 g Mono, 0.9 g Poly, 2.4 g Sat); 13 mg Cholesterol; 5 g Carbohydrate; 1 g Fibre; 4 g Protein; 183 mg Sodium

Pictured at right.

1. Mediterranean Stuffed Peppers, page 19
2. Kasbah Camembert, page 14
3. Grilled Potato Skins, above

Props: Heritage Home

Mediterranean Stuffed Peppers

Colourful little pepper halves are the perfect vessels to hold a Greek-inspired couscous stuffing. Great for entertaining, these peppers can be stuffed and stored in the fridge until ready to grill and serve.

Water	1 cup	250 mL
Whole-wheat couscous	1/2 cup	125 mL
Crumbled feta cheese	1/2 cup	125 mL
Chopped pitted kalamata olives	1/4 cup	60 mL
Finely chopped fresh parsley	1 tbsp.	15 mL
Finely chopped fresh oregano	2 tsp.	10 mL
Garlic clove, minced	1	1
(or 1/4 tsp., 1 mL, powder)		
Grated lemon zest (see Tip, page 50)	1 tsp.	5 mL
Lemon juice	1 tsp.	5 mL
Pepper	1/4 tsp.	1 mL
Baby yellow (or red) peppers, halved lengthwise, stem intact	6	6

Pour water into medium saucepan. Bring to a boil. Add couscous. Stir. Remove from heat. Let stand, covered, for about 5 minutes until liquid is absorbed. Fluff with fork. Transfer to large bowl. Cool for 15 minutes.

Add next 8 ingredients. Stir.

Spoon couscous mixture into pepper halves. Preheat barbecue to medium. Place peppers on greased grill. Close lid. Cook for about 10 minutes until peppers are tender-crisp and skin is starting to blister and blacken. Makes 12 stuffed peppers.

1 stuffed pepper: 48 Calories; 1.8 g Total Fat (0.5 g Mono, 0.1 g Poly, 1.0 g Sat); 6 mg Cholesterol; 7 g Carbohydrate; 1 g Fibre; 2 g Protein; 95 mg Sodium

Pictured on page 17.

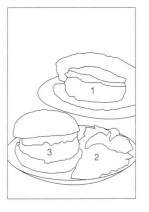

1. Curried Lamb Burgers, page 26
2. Pesto Vegetable Medley, page 132
3. Portobello Chicken Burgers, page 30

Props: Umbra
    Danesco

Tofu "Ceviche"

Pair the fresh citrus and hot chili flavours of ceviche with grilled tofu instead of seafood, and get a refreshing salad packed with flavour for a sunny summer afternoon. Serve with tortilla chips.

Lime juice	3/4 cup	175 mL
Olive oil	1 tbsp.	15 mL
Finely diced fresh hot chili pepper (see Tip, page 150)	2 tsp.	10 mL
Garlic cloves, minced	2	2
Salt	1/2 tsp.	2 mL
Chopped orange segments (1/2 inch, 12 mm, pieces), see Note	1/2 cup	125 mL
Chopped pink grapefruit segments (1/2 inch, 12 mm, pieces), see Note	1/2 cup	125 mL
Diced avocado	1/2 cup	125 mL
Diced English cucumber (with peel)	1/2 cup	125 mL
Finely diced onion	1/4 cup	60 mL
Chopped fresh cilantro (or parsley)	1 tbsp.	15 mL
Package of firm tofu, halved crosswise	12 1/4 oz.	350 g
Soy sauce	1/4 cup	60 mL

Combine first 5 ingredients in small bowl.

Combine next 6 ingredients in medium bowl. Add 1/4 cup (60 mL) lime juice mixture. Stir. Chill.

Cut each tofu piece horizontally into 3 slices. Put into large resealable freezer bag. Add soy sauce to remaining lime juice mixture. Pour over tofu. Seal bag. Turn until coated. Marinate in refrigerator for 2 hours, turning occasionally. Remove tofu. Discard any remaining lime juice mixture. Preheat barbecue to medium-high. Place tofu on well-greased grill. Close lid. Cook for about 4 minutes per side until grill marks appear. Let stand until cool enough to handle. Dice. Add to grapefruit mixture. Toss. Makes about 4 cups (1 L).

1/4 cup (60 mL): 40 Calories; 2.5 g Total Fat (0.7 g Mono, 0.1 g Poly, 0.4 g Sat); 0 mg Cholesterol; 3 g Carbohydrate; 1 g Fibre; 3 g Protein; 134 mg Sodium

Note: To segment citrus, trim a small slice of peel from both ends so the flesh is exposed. Place the fruit, cut-side down, on a cutting board. Remove the peel with a sharp knife, cutting down and around the flesh, leaving as little pith as possible. Over a small bowl, cut on either side of the membranes to release the segments.

20

Grilled Veggie Gazpacho

Gazpacho is Spain's gift to tomato lovers! Grilling intensifies the wonderful flavours of the vegetables in this simple soup that embodies some of the best things about summer.

Roma (plum) tomatoes	4	4
Chopped eggplant (with peel), 1 inch (2.5 cm) pieces	2 cups	500 mL
Chopped zucchini (with peel), 1 inch (2.5 cm) pieces	2 cups	500 mL
Chopped red onion (1 inch, 2.5 cm, pieces)	1 1/2 cups	375 mL
Garlic cloves	4	4
Tomato juice	2 cups	500 mL
Lemon juice	1 tbsp.	15 mL
Granulated sugar	1 tsp.	5 mL
Hot pepper sauce	1/4 tsp.	1 mL
Salt	1/4 tsp.	1 mL
Pepper	1/8 tsp.	0.5 mL
Chopped fresh basil	1 tbsp.	15 mL

Preheat grill basket on barbecue on medium-high. Place tomatoes in greased grill basket. Close lid. Cook for about 10 minutes, turning often, until skins are blistered and blackened. Transfer to small plate. Let stand until cool enough to handle. Remove and discard skin and seeds. Transfer tomatoes to blender or food processor.

Combine next 4 ingredients in same grill basket. Close lid. Cook for about 25 minutes, stirring occasionally, until browned and softened. Add to blender.

Put next 6 ingredients into blender. Carefully process until smooth. Transfer to medium bowl.

Add basil. Stir. Chill. Makes about 5 1/2 cups (1.4 L).

3/4 cup (175 mL): 42 Calories; 0.2 g Total Fat (trace Mono, 0.1 g Poly, trace Sat); 0 mg Cholesterol; 10 g Carbohydrate; 2 g Fibre; 2 g Protein; 246 mg Sodium

Grilled Eggplant Dip

A cousin of baba ganoush, but without the tahini. Garlic complements the smoky flavour of grilled eggplant in this creamy dip.

Medium eggplants (with peel)	2	2
Chopped fresh parsley (or 1 tbsp., 15 mL, dried)	1/4 cup	60 mL
Chopped sun-dried tomatoes	2 tbsp.	30 mL
Olive (or cooking) oil	1 tbsp.	15 mL
Garlic cloves, minced (or 1/2 tsp., 2 mL, powder)	2	2
Lemon juice	2 tsp.	10 mL
Red wine vinegar	1 tsp.	5 mL
Salt	1/2 tsp.	2 mL
Pepper	1/4 tsp.	1 mL
Pita breads (7 inch, 18 cm, diameter)	6	6

Poke several holes randomly with fork into eggplants. Preheat barbecue to medium. Place eggplants on greased grill. Close lid. Cook for about 50 minutes, turning occasionally, until softened and blackened. Transfer to cutting board. Let stand until cool enough to handle. Cut eggplants in half lengthwise. Scoop out flesh into food processor. Discard skins.

Add next 8 ingredients to food processor. Process until smooth.

Place pitas on ungreased grill. Cook for about 1 minute per side until crisp. Transfer to cutting board. Cut each pita into 6 wedges. Serve with eggplant mixture. Makes 36 pita chips and about 3 cups (750 mL) eggplant dip.

1 pita chip with 4 tsp. (20 mL) eggplant dip: 34 Calories; 0.6 g Total Fat (0.3 g Mono, 0.1 g Poly, 0.1 g Sat); 0 mg Cholesterol; 6 g Carbohydrate; trace Fibre; 1 g Protein; 103 mg Sodium

---

Paré Pointer

First he works like a horse, then he hits the hay.

Smoky Grilled Beef Jerky

A tasty appetizer for your guests to munch on with cold beer while the main course is on the grill. A fragrant hickory aroma and savoury spice flavours make these hard to resist.

Soy sauce	1/3 cup	75 mL
Bourbon whiskey	1/4 cup	60 mL
Brown sugar, packed	1/4 cup	60 mL
White vinegar	1/4 cup	60 mL
Worcestershire sauce	2 tbsp.	30 mL
Chili powder	1 tbsp.	15 mL
Garlic powder	1 tbsp.	15 mL
Louisiana hot sauce	2 tsp.	10 mL
Pepper	2 tsp.	10 mL
Flank steak, trimmed of fat, thinly sliced across the grain (1/8 inch, 3 mm, slices), see Note	1 lb.	454 g
Hickory wood chips, soaked in water for 4 hours and drained	2 cups	500 mL

Combine first 9 ingredients in medium bowl.

Put beef into large resealable freezer bag. Pour soy sauce mixture over top. Seal bag. Turn until coated. Marinate in refrigerator for at least 6 hours or overnight, turning occasionally. Remove beef. Discard any remaining soy sauce mixture.

Put wood chips into smoker box. Place smoker box on 1 burner. Turn on burner under smoker box to high. When smoke appears, adjust burner to maintain interior barbecue temperature of medium-low. Arrange beef evenly on sheet of heavy-duty (or double layer of regular) foil. Place on ungreased grill over unlit burner. Close lid. Cook for about 1 hour until darkened. Blot dry with paper towel. Turn beef. Rotate foil 180°. Close lid. Cook for about 2 hours, rotating foil 180° at halftime, until beef is dried but still flexible. Cool completely. Makes about 35 pieces.

1 piece: 25 Calories; 0.9 g Total Fat (0.4 g Mono, trace Poly, 0.4 g Sat); 5 mg Cholesterol; 1 g Carbohydrate; trace Fibre; 3 g Protein; 134 mg Sodium

Note: To slice meat easily, place in freezer for about 30 minutes until just starting to freeze. If using from frozen state, partially thaw before cutting.

Spinach Triangle Breads

Inspired by Middle Eastern fatayer, *or spinach pies, these tasty and fun little triangles are loaded with fresh mint and feta. Serve as part of a Mediterranean meal or with a Greek or fatoush salad for lunch.*

Olive (or cooking) oil	2 tsp.	10 mL
Finely chopped onion	1/2 cup	125 mL
Salt	1/8 tsp.	0.5 mL
Box of frozen chopped spinach, thawed and squeezed dry	10 oz.	300 g
Ground nutmeg	1/8 tsp.	0.5 mL
Pepper	1/8 tsp.	0.5 mL
Crumbled feta cheese	1 cup	250 mL
Chopped fresh mint	2 tbsp.	30 mL
Frozen dinner roll dough, covered, thawed in refrigerator overnight	8	8
Butter (or hard margarine), melted	1 tbsp.	15 mL

Heat olive oil in medium frying pan on medium-high. Add onion and salt. Cook for about 4 minutes, stirring occasionally, until onion is softened and starting to brown.

Add next 3 ingredients. Heat and stir for about 3 minutes until liquid is evaporated. Transfer to large bowl.

Add feta and mint. Stir until well combined. Let stand until cool.

Roll out each dough portion on a lightly floured surface to 5 inch (12.5 cm) circle. Spoon about 1/4 cup (60 mL) spinach mixture in centre of each circle, leaving about 1 inch (2.5 cm) of dough exposed on edges. Fold edges toward centre in 3 sections, leaving centre open, to form a triangle. Pinch corners to seal. Arrange on lightly floured baking sheet. Cover with greased waxed paper and tea towel. Let stand in oven with light on and door closed for about 30 minutes until doubled in size. To preheat barbecue, turn on one burner. Adjust burner to maintain interior barbecue temperature of medium. Transfer dough triangles to greased heavy-duty (or double layer regular) foil over unlit burner. Close lid. Cook for about 20 minutes, rotating foil 180° at halftime, until triangles are golden brown (see Note).

(continued on next page)

Brush with melted butter. Makes 8 triangle breads.

1 triangle bread: 195 Calories; 8.7 g Total Fat (2.1 g Mono, 0.3 g Poly, 3.9 g Sat); 20 mg Cholesterol; 21 g Carbohydrate; 1 g Fibre; 8 g Protein; 559 mg Sodium

Note: You may need to cook these in 2 batches unless you have a very large barbecue.

Mango Salmon Crostini

Combining salmon, hot curry and mango produces an enticing mix of sweet, hot and savoury flavours that come together in a perfect topping for toasted bread. Creamy and refreshing!

Seasoned salt	1/4 tsp.	1 mL
Salmon fillet, skin and any small bones removed	4 oz.	113 g
Plain yogurt	1/4 cup	60 mL
Hot curry paste	1 tbsp.	15 mL
Frozen mango pieces, thawed, chopped	1/2 cup	125 mL
Baguette bread slices (1/2 inch, 12 mm, thick)	16	16
Chopped fresh cilantro (or parsley)	2 tsp.	10 mL

Sprinkle seasoned salt over both sides of fillet. Preheat barbecue to medium-high. Place fillet on well-greased grill. Close lid. Cook for about 3 minutes per side until fish flakes easily when tested with fork. Transfer to plate. Let stand until cool enough to handle. Separate into pieces. Transfer to medium bowl.

Combine yogurt and curry paste in small bowl until smooth. Add mango. Stir. Add to salmon. Stir until well combined.

Place baguette slices on greased grill. Toast for about 1 minute per side until golden. Spoon salmon mixture onto bread slices.

Sprinkle with cilantro. Makes about 16 crostini.

1 crostini: 60 Calories; 1.4 g Total Fat (0.3 g Mono, 0.2 g Poly, 0.3 g Sat); 5 mg Cholesterol; 9 g Carbohydrate; trace Fibre; 3 g Protein; 147 mg Sodium

Curried Lamb Burgers

It might be hard to decide what your favourite part of this dish is—the moist lamb with hints of curry, the crisp, fresh veggies or the tangy yogurt sauce with notes of mint. All of them work together well to create a great burger.

Finely chopped onion	1/2 cup	125 mL
Fine dry bread crumbs	1/4 cup	60 mL
Balkan-style yogurt	2 tbsp.	30 mL
Curry powder	1 tbsp.	15 mL
Tomato paste (see Tip, page 102)	1 tbsp.	15 mL
Salt	1/4 tsp.	1 mL
Lean ground lamb	1 lb.	454 g
Balkan-style yogurt	1/2 cup	125 mL
Chopped fresh mint	2 tbsp.	30 mL
Salt	1/8 tsp.	0.5 mL
Pepper	1/8 tsp.	0.5 mL
Pita breads (7 inch, 18 cm, diameter), see Note	4	4
Thinly sliced English cucumber (with peel)	1 cup	250 mL
Medium tomato, thinly sliced	1	1

Combine first 6 ingredients in medium bowl.

Add lamb. Mix well. Divide into 4 equal portions. Shape into 1 inch (2.5 cm) thick oval-shaped patties. Preheat barbecue to medium. Place patties on greased grill. Close lid. Cook for about 5 minutes per side until internal temperature reaches 160°F (71°C).

Combine next 4 ingredients in small bowl. Spread over pitas.

Place patties over half of each pita. Top with cucumber and tomato. Fold pitas in half to enclose. Makes 4 burgers.

1 burger: 465 Calories; 17.1 g Total Fat (6.6 g Mono, 1.5 g Poly, 6.8 g Sat); 78 mg Cholesterol; 47 g Carbohydrate; 3 g Fibre; 28 g Protein; 688 mg Sodium

Pictured on page 18.

Note: The Indian flatbread *naan* is becoming more common in grocery store bakeries and is a great option in place of the pita. You can warm pita or naan on the grill for about 30 seconds per side, but serve immediately as it will harden quickly.

26 Burgers & More

Chipotle Burgers

This burger is all dressed up with chih-POHT-lay mayo for a trip to sunny California—whatever the local forecast might say!

Mayonnaise	1/3 cup	75 mL
Finely chopped chipotle peppers in adobo sauce (see Tip, page 118)	1 tsp.	5 mL
Grated orange zest	1/2 tsp.	2 mL
Finely chopped red onion	2 tbsp.	30 mL
Crushed seasoned croutons	2 tbsp.	30 mL
Finely chopped chipotle peppers in adobo sauce (see Tip, page 118)	1 tsp.	5 mL
Salt	1/4 tsp.	1 mL
Lean ground beef	1 lb.	454 g
Hamburger buns, split	4	4
Medium avocado, sliced	1	1
Medium tomato slices	4	4
Bacon slices, cooked crisp, cut in half	4	4
Finely shredded fresh basil	1/4 cup	60 mL

Combine first 3 ingredients in small bowl. Chill for 30 minutes to blend flavours.

Combine next 4 ingredients in large bowl.

Add beef. Mix well. Divide into 4 equal portions. Shape into 4 inch (10 cm) patties. Preheat barbecue to medium. Place patties on greased grill. Close lid. Cook for about 7 minutes per side until internal temperature reaches 160°F (71°C).

Spread mayonnaise mixture on bun halves. Serve patties, topped with remaining 4 ingredients, in buns. Makes 4 burgers.

1 burger: 590 Calories; 39.4 g Total Fat (2.3 g Mono, 1.3 g Poly, 9.0 g Sat); 88 mg Cholesterol; 30 g Carbohydrate; 3 g Fibre; 31 g Protein; 779 mg Sodium

Paré Pointer

Kindness always pays the most when you are kind for nothing.

Jerk Pork Patties

These sweet patties get their spicy heat from jerk seasoning and their moistness from bits of mango and red pepper worked right into the meat.

Large egg, fork-beaten	1	1
Frozen mango pieces, thawed and drained, chopped	1 cup	250 mL
Fine dry bread crumbs	1/2 cup	125 mL
Finely chopped onion	1/2 cup	125 mL
Finely chopped red pepper	1/2 cup	125 mL
Jerk seasoning paste	1 1/2 tbsp.	25 mL
Granulated sugar	2 tsp.	10 mL
Ground allspice	1/2 tsp.	2 mL
Salt	1/2 tsp.	2 mL
Pepper	1/4 tsp.	1 mL
Lean ground pork	1 lb.	454 g

Combine first 10 ingredients in large bowl.

Add pork. Mix well. Divide into 4 equal portions. Shape into 4 inch (10 cm) patties. Preheat barbecue to medium. Place patties on greased grill. Close lid. Cook for about 8 minutes per side until internal temperature reaches 160°F (71°C). Makes 4 patties.

1 patty: 422 Calories; 26.1 g Total Fat (10.8 g Mono, 2.2 g Poly, 9.3 g Sat); 135 mg Cholesterol; 23 g Carbohydrate; 2 g Fibre; 23 g Protein; 793 mg Sodium

Beer Brats With Apple Sauerkraut

An ode to Bavaria! These tasty apple and sauerkraut brats will have you reaching for your lederhosen.

Uncooked bratwurst sausages	6	6
Sauerkraut, rinsed and drained	2 cups	500 mL
Thinly sliced onion	1 1/3 cups	325 mL
Thinly sliced tart apple (such as Granny Smith)	1 1/4 cups	300 mL
Warm beer	1 cup	250 mL
Dijon mustard	2 tbsp.	30 mL
Hot dog buns, split	6	6

(continued on next page)

Arrange sausages in single layer in 9 x 9 inch (22 x 22 cm) baking pan. Scatter next 3 ingredients over top.

Combine beer and mustard in medium bowl. Drizzle over sausage mixture. Preheat barbecue to medium. Place pan on ungreased grill. Close lid. Cook for 30 minutes, turning sausages occasionally. Transfer sausages from pan to greased grill. Close lid. Cook sausages, leaving pan on grill, for about 7 minutes per side until browned.

Serve sausages, topped with sauerkraut mixture, in buns. Serves 6.

1 serving: 347 Calories; 15.7 g Total Fat (6.5 g Mono, 2.5 g Poly, 5.3 g Sat); 29 mg Cholesterol; 33 g Carbohydrate; 4 g Fibre; 14 g Protein; 1364 mg Sodium

Mango Chutney Lamb Patties

Mango chutney and lamb are a natural pairing in these rich burgers, which also have feta cheese baked right into the patties. You can eat these on their own or serve them in buns, topped with extra mango chutney mixed with mayonnaise.

Crushed seasoned croutons	1/3 cup	75 mL
Finely chopped onion	1/4 cup	60 mL
Mango chutney, finely chopped	1/4 cup	60 mL
Ground cumin	1/2 tsp.	2 mL
Lean ground lamb	1 lb.	454 g
Crumbled feta cheese	1/3 cup	75 mL
Crushed seasoned croutons	1/3 cup	75 mL
Chopped fresh parsley	1 tbsp.	15 mL
Olive (or cooking) oil	1 tsp.	5 mL

Combine first 4 ingredients in large bowl.

Add lamb. Mix well. Divide into 8 equal portions. Shape into 4 inch (10 cm) patties.

Combine remaining 4 ingredients in small bowl. Divide into 4 equal portions. Spoon feta mixture in centre of 4 patties. Top with remaining 4 patties. Pinch edges to seal. Preheat barbecue to medium. Place patties on greased grill. Close lid. Cook for about 6 minutes per side until internal temperature of lamb reaches 160°F (71°C). Makes 4 patties.

1 patty: 387 Calories; 23.7 g Total Fat (9.5 g Mono, 1.7 g Poly, 9.2 g Sat); 87 mg Cholesterol; 20 g Carbohydrate; 1 g Fibre; 23 g Protein; 570 mg Sodium

Portobello Chicken Burgers

Can't decide whether to make a chicken or a portobello mushroom burger? Have both at the same time! This makes a great alternative to a traditional beef burger.

Portobello mushrooms (about 6 oz., 170 g, each), stems and gills removed (see Note)	4	4
Olive (or cooking) oil	1 tbsp.	15 mL
Salt, sprinkle		
Pepper, sprinkle		
Large egg, fork-beaten	1	1
Grated Parmesan cheese	1/4 cup	60 mL
Fine dry bread crumbs	2 tbsp.	30 mL
Sun-dried tomato pesto	2 tbsp.	30 mL
Finely chopped fresh rosemary	1/4 tsp.	1 mL
Salt	1/4 tsp.	1 mL
Pepper	1/4 tsp.	1 mL
Lean ground chicken	3/4 lb.	340 g
Whole-wheat kaiser rolls, split	4	4
Mayonnaise	1/4 cup	60 mL
Romaine leaves	4	4

Brush mushrooms with olive oil. Sprinkle with salt and pepper. Preheat barbecue to medium. Place mushrooms, stem-side down, on ungreased grill. Close lid. Cook for about 5 minutes until grill marks appear. Transfer, stem-side up, to large plate.

Combine next 7 ingredients in medium bowl.

Add chicken. Mix well. Divide into 4 equal portions. Shape into 4 1/2 inch (11 cm) patties. Press patties firmly into mushrooms. Place on greased grill, patty-side down. Close lid. Cook for about 8 minutes until internal temperature of patty reaches 175°F (80°C). Turn. Close lid. Cook for about 3 minutes until mushroom is tender and browned.

Place roll halves on greased grill. Cook for about 1 minute until golden. Spread mayonnaise on roll halves.

(continued on next page)

Serve patties, topped with lettuce, in rolls. Makes 4 burgers.

1 burger: 492 Calories; 27.1 g Total Fat (3.0 g Mono, 1.5 g Poly, 6.1 g Sat); 123 mg Cholesterol; 37 g Carbohydrate; 7 g Fibre; 27 g Protein; 972 mg Sodium

Pictured on page 18.

Note: Because the gills can sometimes be bitter, be sure to remove them from the portobellos before stuffing. First remove the stems, then, using a small spoon, scrape out and discard the gills.

Grilled Hoisin Patties

If you're hungry for a burger patty that rates high on the flavour meter, try this one. Try serving these patties in buns with slices of grilled pineapple.

Large egg, fork-beaten	1	1
Fine dry bread crumbs	3/4 cup	175 mL
Finely chopped onion	1/2 cup	125 mL
Finely chopped red pepper	1/2 cup	125 mL
Finely chopped celery	1/4 cup	60 mL
Hoisin sauce	3 tbsp.	50 mL
Finely grated ginger root (or 1/2 tsp., 2 mL, ground ginger)	2 tsp.	10 mL
Garlic clove, minced (or 1/4 tsp., 1 mL, powder)	1	1
Extra-lean ground turkey	1 lb.	454 g
Cooking spray		
Hoisin sauce	1/4 cup	60 mL

Combine first 8 ingredients in medium bowl.

Add turkey. Mix well. Divide into 4 equal portions. Shape into 3/4 inch (2 cm) thick patties. Spray both sides of patties with cooking spray.

Preheat barbecue to medium. Place patties on greased grill. Close lid. Cook for 8 minutes per side. Brush with second amount of hoisin sauce. Cook for about 2 minutes per side until browned and internal temperature reaches 175°F (80°C). Makes 4 patties.

1 patty: 294 Calories; 4.4 g Total Fat (trace Mono, 0.1 g Poly, 0.4 g Sat); 99 mg Cholesterol; 34 g Carbohydrate; 2 g Fibre; 33 g Protein; 1191 mg Sodium

Seafood Alfredo Pizza

This one will make you say "wow!" The rustic, hand-formed crust, fresh pesto flavour, abundance of scallops and shrimp and colourful asparagus and pepper combine to make this a delicious showstopper with a coastal vibe.

Loaf of frozen white bread dough, covered, thawed in refrigerator overnight	1	1
Yellow cornmeal, sprinkle		
Olive oil	1 tbsp.	15 mL
Uncooked medium shrimp (peeled and deveined)	3/4 lb.	340 g
Large sea scallops	1/2 lb.	225 g
Bamboo skewers (8 inches, 20 cm, each), soaked in water for 10 minutes	6	6
Fresh asparagus stalks, trimmed of tough ends	16	16
Large orange pepper, cut into 10 rings	1	1
Alfredo pasta sauce	1/2 cup	125 mL
Basil pesto	1 tbsp.	15 mL
Grated Monterey Jack cheese	1 cup	250 mL
Basil pesto	1 tbsp.	15 mL
Lemon juice	1 tbsp.	15 mL

Roll out dough to 10 x 15 inch (25 x 38 cm) rectangle. Transfer to large cutting board sprinkled with cornmeal. Brush with olive oil. To preheat barbecue, turn on one burner. Adjust burner to maintain interior barbecue temperature of medium. Slide dough onto greased grill over lit burner. Cook for about 2 minutes until dough starts to bubble. Turn over onto greased grill over unlit burner.

Thread shrimp and scallops onto skewers. Arrange skewers, asparagus and orange pepper on greased grill over lit burner. Cook for about 1 minute per side until vegetables are tender-crisp, shrimp starts to turn pink and scallops start to turn opaque.

Combine pasta sauce and pesto in small bowl. Brush over dough. Sprinkle with cheese. Arrange asparagus and orange pepper over cheese. Remove shrimp and scallops from skewers. Arrange over asparagus and orange pepper. Turn burner under dough to high. Turn opposite burner off. Close lid. Cook for about 3 minutes until bottom is golden brown. Carefully transfer pizza to cutting board.

(continued on next page)

32 Burgers & More

Combine second amount of pesto and lemon juice in small bowl. Brush over top. Cuts into 6 pieces.

1 piece: 476 Calories; 17.9 g Total Fat (1.8 g Mono, 0.9 g Poly, 5.5 g Sat); 125 mg Cholesterol; 44 g Carbohydrate; 4 g Fibre; 32 g Protein; 850 mg Sodium

Pictured on page 35.

Apple Sage Chicken Burgers

Apple and sage are all the rage in these flavourful chicken burgers.
A subtle sweetness lingers—who would have thought that apple and chicken
would go so well together?

Mayonnaise	1/2 cup	125 mL
Unsweetened applesauce	2 tbsp.	30 mL
Dijon mustard	1 tsp.	5 mL
Large egg, fork-beaten	1	1
Fine dry bread crumbs	1/2 cup	125 mL
Grated havarti cheese	1/4 cup	60 mL
Unsweetened applesauce	2 tbsp.	30 mL
Dijon mustard	2 tsp.	10 mL
Dried sage	1 tsp.	5 mL
Salt	1/2 tsp.	2 mL
Lean ground chicken	1 lb.	454 g
Hamburger buns, split	4	4
Lettuce leaves	4	4

Combine first 3 ingredients in small bowl. Chill.

Combine next 7 ingredients in large bowl.

Add chicken. Mix well. Divide into 4 equal portions. Shape into 4 1/2 inch (11 cm) patties. Preheat barbecue to medium. Place patties on greased grill. Close lid. Cook for about 8 minutes per side until internal temperature reaches 175°F (80°C).

Spread mayonnaise mixture on bun halves. Serve patties, topped with lettuce, in buns. Makes 4 burgers.

1 burger: 581 Calories; 37.3 g Total Fat (0.5 g Mono, 1.0 g Poly, 8.1 g Sat); 145 mg Cholesterol; 33 g Carbohydrate; 2 g Fibre; 27 g Protein; 923 mg Sodium

Pizza Burgers

When you can't decide between serving burgers and serving pizza, you can try this. It looks like a cheeseburger, but tastes like a sausage and pepper pizza! Personalize each burger by adding different toppings.

Large egg, fork-beaten	1	1
Crushed seasoned croutons	1/2 cup	125 mL
Finely chopped onion	1/2 cup	125 mL
Fennel seed	2 tsp.	10 mL
Lean ground beef	1 lb.	454 g
Hot Italian sausage, casing removed	1/2 lb.	225 g
Provolone cheese slices	6	6
Onion buns, split	6	6
Pizza sauce	3/4 cup	175 mL
Small green pepper, cut into 6 rings	1	1
Small red pepper, cut into 6 rings	1	1

Combine first 4 ingredients in medium bowl.

Add beef and sausage. Mix well. Divide into 6 equal portions. Shape into 4 inch (10 cm) patties. Preheat barbecue to medium. Place patties on greased grill. Close lid. Cook for about 5 minutes per side until internal temperature reaches 160°F (71°C).

Place 1 cheese slice on each patty.

Place bun halves on greased grill. Cook for about 1 minute until golden. Spread pizza sauce on bun halves. Serve patties, topped with pepper rings, in buns. Makes 6 burgers.

1 burger: 596 Calories; 30.9 g Total Fat (7.5 g Mono, 1.7 g Poly, 13.3 g Sat); 127 mg Cholesterol; 39 g Carbohydrate; 3 g Fibre; 38 g Protein; 1234 mg Sodium

1. Seafood Alfredo Pizza, page 32

Oktoberfest Burgers

A dish to celebrate the arrival of autumn. Melted cheese, mustard and sauerkraut add great flavour to these sausage-like burgers. Best with beer!

Large egg, fork-beaten	1	1
Rye bread slices, processed into crumbs	1 1/2	1 1/2
Sauerkraut, rinsed and drained	1/2 cup	125 mL
Caraway seed	1/2 tsp.	2 mL
Chopped fresh dill	1/2 tsp.	2 mL
(or 1/8 tsp., 0.5 mL, dried)		
Salt	1/2 tsp.	2 mL
Lean ground beef	1/2 lb.	225 g
Lean ground pork	1/2 lb.	225 g
Swiss cheese slices	4	4
Kaiser rolls, split	4	4
Dijon mustard	8 tsp.	40 mL
Shredded lettuce, lightly packed	1 cup	250 mL

Combine first 6 ingredients in large bowl.

Add beef and pork. Mix well. Divide into 4 equal portions. Shape into 4 1/2 inch (11 cm) patties. Preheat barbecue to medium. Place patties on greased grill. Close lid. Cook for about 7 minutes per side until internal temperature reaches 160°F (71°C). Transfer to large plate.

Top each patty with 1 cheese slice. Cover to keep warm.

Place roll halves on greased grill. Cook for about 1 minute until golden. Spread mustard on bottom half of each roll. Serve patties, topped with lettuce, in rolls. Makes 4 burgers.

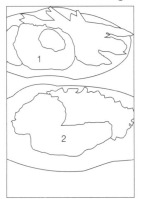

1 burger: 582 Calories; 29.7 g Total Fat (6.2 g Mono, 2.2 g Poly, 12.6 g Sat); 161 mg Cholesterol; 39 g Carbohydrate; 3 g Fibre; 38 g Protein; 1137 mg Sodium

1. Bacon-Wrapped Filet Mignon, page 50
2. Curry-Stuffed Steaks, page 51

Props: Stokes

Chicken Souvlaki Pitas

Chicken souvlaki meets Greek salad. These two favourites are rolled up in one big sloppy pita!

Boneless, skinless chicken breast halves, cut into 24 pieces	1 lb.	454 g
Bamboo skewers (8 inches, 20 cm, each), soaked in water for 10 minutes	4	4
Lemon juice	1/4 cup	60 mL
Olive (or cooking) oil	2 tbsp.	30 mL
Grated lemon zest (see Tip, page 50)	2 tsp.	10 mL
Dried oregano	1 tsp.	5 mL
Garlic cloves, minced (or 1/2 tsp., 2 mL, powder)	2	2
Salt	1/2 tsp.	2 mL
Pepper	1 tsp.	5 mL
Tzatziki	1/4 cup	60 mL
Black olive tapenade	2 tbsp.	30 mL
Pita breads (7 inch, 18 cm, diameter)	4	4
Sliced tomato	2/3 cup	150 mL
Thinly sliced English cucumber (with peel)	1/2 cup	125 mL
Crumbled feta cheese	1/2 cup	125 mL
Julienned yellow pepper	1/4 cup	60 mL
Thinly sliced red onion	1/4 cup	60 mL

Thread chicken onto skewers. Place in large shallow dish.

Combine next 7 ingredients in small bowl. Pour over chicken. Turn until coated. Marinate, covered, in refrigerator for 2 hours, turning occasionally. Remove skewers. Discard any remaining lemon juice mixture. Preheat barbecue to medium-high. Place skewers on greased grill. Close lid. Cook for about 12 minutes, turning occasionally, until chicken is no longer pink inside.

Combine tzatziki and tapenade in small bowl. Place pitas on greased grill. Heat for about 30 seconds until softened. Spread with tzatziki mixture. Remove chicken from skewers and arrange across centre of each pita.

Top with remaining 5 ingredients. Fold pitas in half to enclose filling. Secure with wooden picks. Serve immediately. Makes 4 pitas.

(continued on next page)

1 pita: 410 Calories; 11.8 g Total Fat (3.8 g Mono, 1.3 g Poly, 4.4 g Sat); 82 mg Cholesterol; 39 g Carbohydrate; 2 g Fibre; 35 g Protein; 843 mg Sodium

Pictured on page 71.

Pesto Chicken Cheeseburgers

Here's something different for a late-afternoon barbecue. Dressed with tomato, basil pesto and melted provolone cheese, this burger steps out of the ordinary.

Basil pesto	1/3 cup	75 mL
Mayonnaise	1/4 cup	60 mL
Large egg, fork-beaten	1	1
Fine dry bread crumbs	1/2 cup	125 mL
Finely chopped onion	1/3 cup	75 mL
Dried oregano	1/4 tsp.	1 mL
Salt	1/2 tsp.	2 mL
Pepper	1/8 tsp.	0.5 mL
Lean ground chicken	1 1/2 lbs.	680 g
Large tomato slices	6	6
Provolone (or mozzarella) cheese slices	6	6
Hamburger buns, split	6	6

Combine pesto and mayonnaise in small bowl. Chill.

Combine next 6 ingredients in large bowl.

Add chicken. Mix well. Divide into 6 equal portions. Shape into 4 inch (10 cm) patties.

Preheat barbecue to medium. Place patties on greased grill. Close lid. Cook for about 7 minutes per side until internal temperature reaches 175°F (80°C). Place 1 tomato slice on each patty. Top with 1 cheese slice. Cook for about 2 minutes until cheese is melted.

Spread pesto mixture on bun halves. Serve patties in buns. Makes 6 cheeseburgers.

1 cheeseburger: 564 Calories; 33.9 g Total Fat (2.6 g Mono, 1.1 g Poly, 10.2 g Sat); 137 mg Cholesterol; 31 g Carbohydrate; 2 g Fibre; 34 g Protein; 963 mg Sodium

Super Veggie Burgers

A fragrant beet relish adds colour and pungent flavour to these nutty-tasting open-faced burgers. So good that they will easily appeal to vegetarians and meat-lovers alike.

BEET RELISH

Sliced pickled beets, drained	1 cup	250 mL
Prepared horseradish	1 tbsp.	15 mL
Cooking oil	2 tsp.	10 mL
Ground cloves, just a pinch		

VEGGIE BURGERS

Falafel mix, stir before measuring	1 cup	250 mL
Water	1/2 cup	125 mL
Large egg, fork-beaten	1	1
Cooked long-grain brown rice	1 cup	250 mL
(about 1/4 cup, 60 mL, uncooked)		
Salted, roasted sunflower seeds	1/2 cup	125 mL
Fine dry bread crumbs	1/4 cup	60 mL
Mayonnaise	2 tbsp.	30 mL
Chopped fresh thyme	1 tsp.	5 mL
(or 1/4 tsp., 1 mL, dried)		
Mayonnaise	2 tbsp.	30 mL
Prepared horseradish	1/2 tsp.	2 mL
Whole-wheat Kaiser rolls, split	2	2
Shredded romaine lettuce, lightly packed	1 cup	250 mL

Beet Relish: Process all 4 ingredients in blender until finely chopped. Makes about 3/4 cup (175 mL).

Veggie Burgers: Combine falafel mix and water in medium bowl. Add next 6 ingredients. Mix well. Divide into 4 equal portions. Shape into 4 inch (10 cm) patties. Chill, covered, for 1 hour. Preheat barbecue to medium. Arrange patties on sheet of greased heavy-duty (or double layer of regular) foil. Place on ungreased grill. Close lid. Cook for about 7 minutes per side until browned.

Combine mayonnaise and second amount of horseradish in small cup.

(continued on next page)

Place roll halves on greased grill. Cook for about 1 minute until golden. Spread mayonnaise mixture on roll halves.

Arrange lettuce over mayonnaise mixture. Place patties over lettuce. Top with Beet Relish. Makes 4 veggie burgers.

1 veggie burger: 568 Calories; 30.2 g Total Fat (1.8 g Mono, 1.4 g Poly, 3.7 g Sat); 59 mg Cholesterol; 61 g Carbohydrate; 10 g Fibre; 16 g Protein; 875 mg Sodium

Mango Brie Quesadillas

Sweet mango, creamy brie and caramelized onion elevate a simple quesadilla to something quite sophisticated and extraordinary. Try these with sun-dried tomato tortillas for a boost of colour and flavour.

Olive (or cooking) oil	2 tsp.	10 mL
Thinly sliced sweet onion	1 cup	250 mL
Salt	1/4 tsp.	1 mL
Pepper	1/4 tsp.	1 mL
Brown sugar, packed	1 tsp.	5 mL
White wine vinegar	1/2 tsp.	2 mL
Thinly sliced ripe mango	3/4 cup	175 mL
Brie cheese round, thinly sliced	4 oz.	125 g
Flour tortillas (9 inch, 22 cm, diameter)	4	4

Cooking spray

Heat olive oil in medium frying pan on medium. Add next 3 ingredients. Cook for about 5 minutes, stirring often, until onion is softened.

Add brown sugar and vinegar. Cook for about 10 minutes, stirring often, until onion starts to brown.

Arrange mango slices and cheese over half of each tortilla. Spoon onion mixture over top. Fold tortillas in half to cover filling. Press down lightly.

Spray both sides of each tortilla with cooking spray. Preheat barbecue to medium. Place tortillas on greased grill. Close lid. Cook for about 5 minutes per side until cheese is melted and grill marks appear. Cut each quesadilla into 4 wedges. Makes 16 wedges.

1 wedge: 73 Calories; 3.7 g Total Fat (1.0 g Mono, 0.2 g Poly, 1.6 g Sat); 7 mg Cholesterol; 8 g Carbohydrate; trace Fibre; 2 g Protein; 160 mg Sodium

Asian Shrimp Po'boys

This open-faced po'boy is loosely based on a Vietnamese banh-mi *sandwich, making it a blend of flavours from many cultures. Wasabi adds pleasant heat and grilled suey choy adds a subtle smoky flavour.*

Mayonnaise	2/3 cup	150 mL
Finely chopped pickled ginger slices	1 tbsp.	15 mL
Lime juice	1 tbsp.	15 mL
Soy sauce	2 tsp.	10 mL
Wasabi paste (Japanese horseradish)	1 tsp.	5 mL
Sesame oil (for flavour)	1/2 tsp.	2 mL
Medium suey choy (Chinese cabbage), halved lengthwise	1/2	1/2
Sesame oil (for flavour)	1 tbsp.	15 mL
Cooking oil	1/4 cup	60 mL
Ground ginger	1/4 tsp.	1 mL
Salt	1/4 tsp.	1 mL
Pepper	1/8 tsp.	0.5 mL
Uncooked medium shrimp (peeled and deveined)	1 lb.	454 g
Bamboo skewers (8 inches, 20 cm, each), soaked in water for 10 minutes	10	10
Baguette bread loaf, split	1/2	1/2

Combine first 6 ingredients in small bowl. Chill.

Brush suey choy with second amount of sesame oil. Preheat barbecue to medium-high. Place suey choy on greased grill. Cook for about 2 minutes per side until grill marks appear. Remove and discard core. Slice thinly. Transfer to medium bowl.

Combine next 4 ingredients in separate medium bowl.

Add shrimp. Toss until coated. Thread shrimp onto doubled skewers (see Tip, page 56). Place on greased grill. Cook for 2 minutes per side until shrimp turn pink. Remove shrimp from skewers. Add to suey choy mixture. Add mayonnaise mixture. Toss.

Cut bread loaf half in half crosswise. Remove soft bread from centre of each piece, leaving 1/2 inch (12 mm) shell. Spoon shrimp mixture into shells. Makes 4 po'boys.

1 po'boy: 644 Calories; 50.4 g Total Fat (8.3 g Mono, 4.9 g Poly, 6.0 g Sat); 188 mg Cholesterol; 21 g Carbohydrate; 2 g Fibre; 28 g Protein; 1033 mg Sodium

Caprese Burgers

Fresh ingredients are what make the Caprese salad, from the island of Capri, famous. They're combined in a new way in this recipe to make this burger delicious. The simple, natural flavours of the key ingredients really shine through.

Mayonnaise	1/4 cup	60 mL
Chopped fresh basil	1 tbsp.	15 mL
Garlic clove, minced (or 1/4 tsp., 1 mL, powder)	1	1
Balsamic vinegar	1/4 tsp.	1 mL
Large egg, fork-beaten	1	1
Fresh bread crumbs	1/3 cup	75 mL
Finely chopped onion	1/4 cup	60 mL
Garlic clove, minced (or 1/4 tsp., 1 mL, powder)	1	1
Salt	1/2 tsp.	2 mL
Pepper	1/2 tsp.	2 mL
Lean ground beef	1 lb.	454 g
Mozzarella cheese slices (3 inch, 7.5 cm, squares)	4	4
Ciabatta rolls, split	4	4
Arugula, lightly packed	1 cup	250 mL
Medium tomato, thinly sliced	1	1

Combine first 4 ingredients in small bowl. Chill.

Combine next 6 ingredients in medium bowl.

Add beef. Mix well. Divide into 8 equal portions. Shape into 4 inch (10 cm) patties.

Place cheese slices in centres of 4 patties. Top with remaining 4 patties. Pinch edges to seal. Preheat barbecue to medium. Place patties on greased grill. Close lid. Cook for about 8 minutes per side until internal temperature reaches 160°F (71°C).

Place roll halves on greased grill. Toast for about 1 minute until golden. Spread mayonnaise mixture on roll halves.

Arrange arugula on bottom halves of rolls. Serve patties, topped with tomato, in rolls. Makes 4 burgers.

1 burger: 720 Calories; 30.9 g Total Fat (0 g Mono, trace Poly, 10.4 g Sat); 147 mg Cholesterol; 64 g Carbohydrate; 2 g Fibre; 43 g Protein; 1273 mg Sodium

Bruschetta Steak Sandwiches

Roasted tomatoes and a sweet-and-sour herb sauce combine with succulent steak for an explosion of flavours in every bite.

Medium tomatoes, halved crosswise	4	4
Cooking oil	1/4 cup	60 mL
Finely chopped onion	1/4 cup	60 mL
Garlic cloves, minced	3	3
Salt	3/4 tsp.	4 mL
Chopped fresh mint (or 1 1/2 tsp., 7 mL, dried)	2 tbsp.	30 mL
Beef strip loin steaks (3/4 inch, 2 cm, thick)	1 lb.	454 g
Salt	1/2 tsp.	2 mL
Pepper	1/2 tsp.	2 mL
Sourdough bread slices (1/2 inch, 12 mm, thick)	4	4
Cooking oil	1 tsp.	5 mL
Red wine vinegar	1 tbsp.	15 mL
Granulated sugar	1 tsp.	5 mL
Fresh spinach leaves, lightly packed	1 1/2 cups	375 mL

Arrange tomato halves, cut-side up, in greased 9 inch (22 cm) foil pie plate. Combine next 4 ingredients in small bowl. Spoon over tomatoes. Preheat barbecue to medium-high. Place pie plate on ungreased grill. Close lid. Cook for about 20 minutes until tomatoes are tender. Let stand until cool enough to handle. Chop. Transfer to small bowl.

Add mint. Stir.

Sprinkle both sides of each steak with salt and pepper. Place steaks on greased grill. Close lid. Cook for about 4 minutes per side until internal temperature reaches 145°F (63°C) for medium-rare or until steaks reach desired doneness. Transfer to cutting board. Cover with foil. Let stand for 10 minutes. Cut diagonally across the grain into thin slices.

Brush bread slices on both sides with second amount of cooking oil. Place on greased grill. Toast for about 30 seconds per side until golden.

Stir vinegar and sugar in medium bowl until sugar is dissolved. Add spinach. Toss. Arrange spinach mixture on bread slices. Top with beef and tomato mixture. Makes 4 sandwiches.

(continued on next page)

1 sandwich: 519 Calories; 24.2 g Total Fat (12.1 g Mono, 5.1 g Poly, 4.0 g Sat); 49 mg Cholesterol; 44 g Carbohydrate; 3 g Fibre; 32 g Protein; 1181 mg Sodium

Pictured on page 126.

─────

Dilled Salmon Burgers

Light, fresh lemon and dill make this a burger to rival the best. Great on a hot day with a light green salad and a chilled crisp white wine.

Large egg	1	1
Fine dry bread crumbs	1/3 cup	75 mL
Chopped fresh dill	1 tbsp.	15 mL
(or 1 1/2 tsp., 7 mL, dried)		
Dijon mustard	1 tbsp.	15 mL
Salt	1/2 tsp.	2 mL
Pepper	1/2 tsp.	2 mL
Salmon fillets, skin and any small bones removed, cut into 1 inch (2.5 cm) pieces	1 lb.	454 g
Sour cream	1/2 cup	125 mL
Chopped fresh dill	2 tbsp.	30 mL
(or 1 1/2 tsp., 7 mL, dried)		
Grated lemon zest	1 tsp.	5 mL
Hamburger buns, split	4	4
Sliced red onion	1/4 cup	60 mL
Butter lettuce leaves	8	8

Put first 6 ingredients into food processor. Pulse with on/off motion until combined.

Add salmon. Pulse with on/off motion until coarsely ground. Divide into 4 equal portions. Shape into 4 inch (10 cm) patties. Chill, covered, for 1 hour. Preheat barbecue to medium. Place salmon patties on greased grill. Close lid. Cook for about 6 minutes per side until internal temperature reaches 160°F (71°C).

Combine next 3 ingredients in small bowl.

Place bun halves on greased grill. Toast for about 1 minute until golden. Spread sour cream mixture on bun halves. Serve patties, topped with onion and lettuce, in buns. Makes 4 burgers.

1 burger: 445 Calories; 20.4 g Total Fat (5.5 g Mono, 4.1 g Poly, 7.9 g Sat); 130 mg Cholesterol; 31 g Carbohydrate; 2 g Fibre; 31 g Protein; 697 mg Sodium

Company's Coming Pizzas

Need to feed a crowd but don't want to spend the whole time in the kitchen?
Prep and pre-grill individual crusts before your guests arrive and then let
everyone add their own favourite toppings to finish on the barbecue. Great for
a hot summer day when you just don't want to turn the oven on!

Warm water	1 1/2 cups	375 mL
Granulated sugar	1 tsp.	5 mL
Package of active dry yeast	1/4 oz.	8 g
(or 2 1/4 tsp., 11 mL)		
Olive (or cooking) oil	1 tbsp.	15 mL
All-purpose flour	3 1/2 cups	875 mL
Whole-wheat flour	1 cup	250 mL
Italian seasoning	2 tsp.	10 mL
Salt	2 tsp.	10 mL
Pizza sauce	2/3 cup	150 mL
Grated Mexican cheese blend	1 1/2 cups	375 mL

Stir water and sugar in medium bowl until sugar is dissolved. Sprinkle yeast
over top. Let stand for 10 minutes. Stir until yeast is dissolved.

Add olive oil. Stir.

Combine next 4 ingredients in large bowl. Add yeast mixture. Mix until
soft dough forms. Turn out onto lightly floured surface. Knead for about
8 minutes until smooth and elastic. Place in greased large bowl, turning
once to grease top. Cover with greased waxed paper and tea towel. Let
stand in oven with light on and door closed for about 1 hour until doubled
in bulk. Punch dough down. Turn out onto lightly floured surface. Knead for
about 1 minute until smooth. Divide into 10 equal portions. Roll out each
portion on lightly floured surface to 6 inch (15 cm) circle. Preheat barbecue
to high. Place pizza crusts, 2 or 3 at a time, on greased grill. Cook for about
2 minutes per side until light grill marks appear. Cool. Poke several holes
randomly with fork into each pizza crust.

Spread 1 tbsp. (15 mL) pizza sauce over each pizza crust. Sprinkle with
1/4 cup (60 mL) cheese. Preheat barbecue to medium. Place pizzas, 2 or
3 at a time, on greased grill. Close lid. Cook for 8 to 12 minutes until
toppings are heated through and cheese is melted. Makes 10 pizzas.

1 pizza: 273 Calories; 7.3 g Total Fat (1.1 g Mono, 0.3 g Poly, 3.3 g Sat); 15 mg Cholesterol;
42 g Carbohydrate; 3 g Fibre; 10 g Protein; 643 mg Sodium

(continued on next page)

MARGHERITA PIZZA: Use pizza sauce. For toppings, use sliced fresh tomatoes and Italian cheese blend. Sprinkle with chopped fresh basil to serve.

VEGETARIAN PIZZA: Use pizza sauce and basil pesto for sauce. For toppings, use thinly sliced green peppers, thinly sliced red onion, thinly sliced mushrooms, thinly sliced fresh tomatoes, Italian cheese blend and chopped fresh oregano.

DELI PIZZA: Use pizza sauce. For toppings, use ham, pepperoni, salami, chopped cooked bacon, Mexican cheese blend and chopped fresh parsley.

TOP-CRUST PIZZA: Use basil pesto for pizza sauce. For toppings, use thinly sliced mushrooms, thinly sliced red onion, chopped cooked bacon and crumbled blue cheese.

FAJITA PIZZA: Use salsa for pizza sauce. For toppings, use finely chopped cooked chicken, thinly sliced red onion, thinly sliced red peppers and Mexican cheese blend. Sprinkle with chopped fresh cilantro to serve.

Paré Pointer
The early bird may get the worm but it's the second mouse that gets the cheese.

(15) Ooey Gooey Chewy Panini

Ready in 15 minutes

An old favourite gets a classy update. This cheese sandwich, made with crispy sourdough and filled with sharp Swiss and creamy Havarti, really is grilled and tastes like it just came, made-to-order, off a panini press.

Havarti cheese slices	4	4
Swiss cheese slices	4	4
Sourdough bread slices	4	4
(1/2 inch, 12 mm, thick)		
Butter, melted	2 tbsp.	30 mL
Finely chopped fresh rosemary	1/2 tsp.	2 mL
(or 1/8 tsp., 0.5 mL, dried, crushed)		
Cayenne pepper, sprinkle		
Salt, sprinkle		
Pepper, sprinkle		
Grated Parmesan cheese	2 tbsp.	30 mL

Arrange havarti and Swiss cheese on 2 bread slices. Cover with remaining bread slices.

Combine next 5 ingredients in small bowl. Brush 1 tbsp. (15 mL) over tops of sandwiches.

Sprinkle with 1 tbsp. (15 mL) Parmesan cheese. Press down lightly. Preheat barbecue to medium. Place sandwiches on greased grill, cheese-side down. Place a baking sheet with bricks or heavy weights over sandwiches. Close lid. Cook for about 3 minutes until golden. Brush tops of sandwiches with remaining butter mixture. Sprinkle with remaining Parmesan cheese. Press down lightly. Turn. Place baking sheet with weight over sandwiches. Close lid. Cook for about 3 minutes until cheese is melted and bread is golden. Transfer to cutting board. Cut each sandwich in half. Makes 4 panini.

1 panini: 461 Calories; 25.8 g Total Fat (2.3 g Mono, 0.7 g Poly, 15.8 g Sat); 74 mg Cholesterol; 34 g Carbohydrate; 2 g Fibre; 23 g Protein; 724 mg Sodium

Pictured on page 72.

Paré Pointer

Pilots have lots of room for their belongings. They use air pockets.

Chili Pork Fajitas

Have the fun of going out for Mexican food—without going any further than your barbecue. These build-your-own tortilla wraps, filled with subtly spiced pork and smoky-sweet grilled veggies, are better than any restaurant fare!

Coarsely chopped fresh cilantro (or parsley)	1/2 cup	125 mL
Olive (or cooking) oil	1/4 cup	60 mL
Lime juice	2 tbsp.	30 mL
Chili powder	2 tsp.	10 mL
Ground cumin	1/2 tsp.	2 mL
Sour cream	1/2 cup	125 mL
Boneless centre-cut pork chops	1 lb.	454 g
Salt, sprinkle		
Pepper, sprinkle		
Large red onion, cut crosswise into 1/4 inch (6 mm) slices	1	1
Large yellow (or red) peppers, cut lengthwise into 3/4 inch (2 cm) slices	3	3
Flour tortillas (9 inch, 22 cm, diameter)	6	6

Process first 5 ingredients in blender or food processor until smooth.

Put sour cream in small cup. Add 1 tbsp. (15 mL) cilantro mixture. Stir. Chill.

Sprinkle both sides of pork chops with salt and pepper. Preheat barbecue to medium. Place chops on greased grill. Close lid. Cook for about 4 minutes per side until internal temperature reaches 155°F (68°C). Transfer to cutting board. Cover with foil. Let stand for 10 minutes. Internal temperature should rise to at least 160°F (71°C). Cut into thin slices. Transfer to medium bowl. Add 2 tbsp. (30 mL) cilantro mixture. Toss.

Place onion and peppers on greased grill. Close lid. Cook for about 15 minutes, turning often and brushing with remaining cilantro mixture, until tender.

Place tortillas on greased grill. Cook for about 30 seconds per side until heated through. Spread sour cream mixture on 1 side of each tortilla. Arrange pork mixture down centre of each tortilla. Top with onion and pepper. Fold bottom end of tortilla over filling. Fold in sides, leaving top end open. Makes 6 fajitas.

1 fajita: 398 Calories; 21.5 g Total Fat (8.7 g Mono, 1.8 g Poly, 6.2 g Sat); 61 mg Cholesterol; 31 g Carbohydrate; 1 g Fibre; 21 g Protein; 350 mg Sodium

Bacon-Wrapped Filet Mignon

Lemon parsley butter adds extra moisture and flavour to tender filet mignon without overpowering the meat. And it's wrapped in bacon. Yum!

LEMON PARSLEY BUTTER

Butter, softened	3 tbsp.	50 mL
Chopped fresh parsley	1 tbsp.	15 mL
Lemon juice	1/2 tsp.	2 mL
Grated lemon zest (see Tip, below)	1/4 tsp.	1 mL
Salt	1/4 tsp.	1 mL
Pepper	1/4 tsp.	1 mL

BACON-WRAPPED FILETS

Bacon slices	4	4
Beef tenderloin steaks (4 – 5 oz., 113 – 140 g each), about 1 1/2 inches (3.8 cm) thick	4	4
Salt	1/2 tsp.	2 mL
Pepper	1/2 tsp.	2 mL

Lemon Parsley Butter: Beat all 6 ingredients in small bowl until combined. Transfer to sheet of waxed paper. Form into 2 inch (5 cm) long log. Wrap in waxed paper. Chill for at least 1 hour until firm. Remove waxed paper. Cut into 4 slices. Makes about 3 tbsp. (50 mL).

Bacon-Wrapped Filets: Wrap 1 bacon slice around edge of each steak. Secure with wooden pick. Sprinkle both sides of each steak with salt and pepper. Preheat barbecue to medium-high. Place steaks on greased grill. Close lid. Cook for about 8 minutes per side until internal temperature reaches 145°F (63°C) for medium-rare or until steaks reach desired doneness. Transfer to large plate. Cover with foil. Let stand for 10 minutes. Remove and discard wooden picks. Top each steak with slice of Lemon Parsley Butter. Serves 4.

1 serving: 231 Calories; 15.2 g Total Fat (4.9 g Mono, 0.6 g Poly, 7.8 g Sat); 90 mg Cholesterol; trace Carbohydrate; trace Fibre; 25 g Protein; 698 mg Sodium

Pictured on page 36.

 tip When a recipe calls for grated zest and juice, it's easier to grate the fruit first, then juice it. Be careful not to grate down to the pith (white part of the peel), which is bitter and best avoided.

Curry-Stuffed Steaks

Here's a unique way to dress up a steak—fill it with a warmly spiced curried fruit mix reminiscent of Moroccan cuisine. A side of couscous makes for an elegant presentation.

Hot water	1 cup	250 mL
Dark raisins	1/2 cup	125 mL
Dried apricots, chopped	1/4 cup	60 mL
Slivered almonds, toasted (see Tip, page 86)	1/4 cup	60 mL
Plain yogurt	3 tbsp.	50 mL
Hot curry paste	1 tbsp.	15 mL
Beef strip loin steaks (about 1 inch, 2.5 cm, thick)	4	4
Ground cinnamon	1/2 tsp.	2 mL
Ground cumin	1/2 tsp.	2 mL
Salt	1/2 tsp.	2 mL
Pepper	1/4 tsp.	1 mL

Combine first 3 ingredients in small bowl. Let stand, covered, for about 15 minutes until fruit is plump. Drain.

Add next 3 ingredients. Stir well.

Cut horizontal slits in steaks to create pockets. Fill with fruit mixture. Secure with wooden picks.

Combine remaining 4 ingredients in small cup. Sprinkle both sides of steaks with cinnamon mixture. Preheat barbecue to medium-high. Place steaks on greased grill. Close lid. Cook for about 5 minutes per side until internal temperature of steak (not stuffing) reaches 145°F (63°C) for medium-rare or until steaks reach desired doneness. Transfer to large plate. Cover with foil. Let stand for 10 minutes. Remove and discard wooden picks. Makes 4 stuffed steaks.

1 stuffed steak: 661 Calories; 27.6 g Total Fat (11.7 g Mono, 1.7 g Poly, 9.7 g Sat); 175 mg Cholesterol; 24 g Carbohydrate; 3 g Fibre; 74 g Protein; 583 mg Sodium

Pictured on page 36.

Meat and Potato Skewers

Barbecuing shouldn't just be for grown-ups. These skewers are fun, easy and a big hit with the kids.

Red baby potatoes, larger ones halved	16	16
Frozen cooked meatballs, thawed	24	24
Large red pepper, cut into 24 equal pieces	1	1
Bamboo skewers (8 inches, 20 cm, each), soaked in water for 10 minutes	16	16
Peppercorn ranch dressing	1/2 cup	125 mL

Pour water into medium saucepan until about 1 inch (2.5 cm) deep. Add potatoes. Cover. Bring to a boil. Reduce heat to medium. Boil gently for 12 to 15 minutes until potatoes are tender. Drain. Let stand until cool enough to handle.

Thread potatoes, meatballs and peppers alternately onto doubled skewers (see Tip, page 56).

Preheat barbecue to medium-high. Place skewers on greased grill. Close lid. Cook for about 10 minutes, turning occasionally and brushing with 1/4 cup (60 mL) dressing, until browned and heated through. Serve with remaining dressing. Makes 8 skewers.

1 skewer: 381 Calories; 27.6 g Total Fat (0 g Mono, trace Poly, 9.1 g Sat); 44 mg Cholesterol; 17 g Carbohydrate; 3 g Fibre; 5 g Protein; 887 mg Sodium

Pictured at right.

1. Curried Chicken Kabobs, page 78
2. Mirin Wasabi Tuna Skewers, page 94
3. Meat and Potato Skewers, above

Props: La Dolce Vita

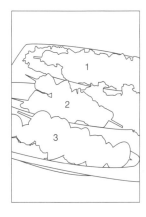

Dad's Grilled Meatloaf

Mom's traditional meatloaf is always made in the oven, but if Dad had his way, he would probably cook it on the barbecue! The tangy sweet-and-sour sauce makes a great accompaniment to this moist loaf.

Large egg, fork-beaten	1	1
Fine dry bread crumbs	1/2 cup	125 mL
Finely chopped onion	1/2 cup	125 mL
Bacon slices, chopped	6	6
Montreal steak spice	1 tbsp.	15 mL
Lean ground beef	2 lbs.	900 g
Ketchup	1/2 cup	125 mL
Brown sugar, packed	3 tbsp.	50 mL
Apple cider vinegar	1 tbsp.	15 mL
Hot pepper sauce	1 tsp.	5 mL

Combine first 5 ingredients in medium bowl.

Add beef. Mix well. Shape into 7 inch (18 cm) round loaf. Place in 9 inch (22 cm) foil pie plate. To preheat barbecue, turn on one burner. Adjust burner to maintain interior barbecue temperature of medium. Place pie plate on ungreased grill over unlit burner. Close lid. Cook for 1 hour.

Combine remaining 4 ingredients in small bowl. Reserve 1/3 cup (75 mL). Remove meatloaf from pan. Place on greased grill over unlit burner. Spread remaining ketchup mixture over meatloaf. Close lid. Cook for about 15 minutes until internal temperature reaches 160°F (71°C). Serve with reserved ketchup mixture. Cuts into 8 slices. Serves 8.

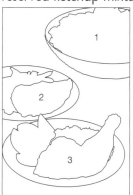

1 serving: 310 Calories; 14.3 g Total Fat (0.9 g Mono, 0.2 g Poly, 5.5 g Sat); 106 mg Cholesterol; 18 g Carbohydrate; trace Fibre; 26 g Protein; 598 mg Sodium

1. Avocado Lime Turkey Salad, page 69
2. Smoky Grilled Chicken, page 67
3. Grilled Citrus Chicken, page 68

Props: Inspired Solar

Mushroom Meatball Skewers

These earthy, mushroom-flavoured meatballs can be served on their own,
brushed with your favourite sauce or served with your favourite dip.

Package of dried porcini mushrooms	3/4 oz.	22 g
Boiling water	1 cup	250 mL
Fine dry bread crumbs	1/4 cup	60 mL
Dried basil	1 tsp.	5 mL
Garlic clove, minced	1	1
(or 1/4 tsp., 1 mL, powder)		
Dried thyme	1/2 tsp.	2 mL
Salt	1/2 tsp.	2 mL
Pepper	1/4 tsp.	1 mL
Lean ground beef	1 lb.	454 g
Bamboo skewers (8 inches, 20 cm, each)	8	8
soaked in water for 10 minutes		

Combine dried mushrooms and boiling water in small heatproof bowl. Let stand for 10 minutes. Remove and discard 1/3 cup (75 mL) liquid. Process mushrooms and remaining liquid in blender or food processor until finely chopped. Transfer to large bowl.

Add next 6 ingredients. Stir.

Add beef. Mix well. Roll into 1 1/4 inch (3 cm) balls. Makes about 24 meatballs. Chill for 30 minutes.

Thread meatballs onto doubled skewers (see Tip, below). Preheat barbecue to medium. Place skewers on greased grill. Close lid. Cook for about 18 minutes, turning occasionally, until meatballs are no longer pink inside. Makes 4 skewers.

1 skewer: 246 Calories; 11.8 g Total Fat (trace Mono, trace Poly, 4.7 g Sat); 74 mg Cholesterol;
9 g Carbohydrate; 1 g Fibre; 24 g Protein; 419 mg Sodium

 tip When grilling skewered ingredients, use doubled skewers to prevent ingredients from rotating when turning.

Ginger Beef Steaks

Tired of those tough strips of ginger-fried beef? We've paired the classic flavours of ginger and beef in a new and tasty way. Tender, juicy strip loin steak is glazed in a soy and ginger marmalade reduction.

Prepared vegetable broth	1/2 cup	125 mL
Soy sauce	1/4 cup	60 mL
Brown sugar, packed	2 tbsp.	30 mL
Rice vinegar	2 tbsp.	30 mL
Sesame oil (for flavour)	2 tbsp.	30 mL
Garlic cloves, minced	4	4
Finely grated ginger root	1 tbsp.	15 mL
Pepper	1/2 tsp.	2 mL
Beef strip loin steaks (about 3/4 inch, 2 cm, thick)	4	4
Ginger marmalade	1/3 cup	75 mL

Combine first 8 ingredients in small bowl.

Place steaks in large resealable freezer bag. Pour broth mixture over top. Seal bag. Turn until coated. Marinate in refrigerator for 4 hours, turning occasionally. Remove steaks. Transfer broth mixture to medium saucepan.

Add marmalade. Stir. Bring to a boil. Reduce heat to medium. Boil, uncovered, for about 10 minutes, stirring occasionally, until thickened to syrup consistency. Reserve 1/3 cup (75 mL). Preheat barbecue to medium-high. Place steaks on greased grill. Close lid. Cook for about 5 minutes per side, brushing occasionally with remaining marmalade mixture, until internal temperature reaches 145°F (63°C) for medium-rare or until steaks reach desired doneness. Transfer to large plate. Cover with foil. Let stand for 10 minutes. Serve with reserved marmalade mixture. Makes 4 steaks.

1 steak: 553 Calories; 32.7 g Total Fat (11.0 g Mono, 1.0 g Poly, 11.3 g Sat); 94 mg Cholesterol; 28 g Carbohydrate; trace Fibre; 37 g Protein; 1480 mg Sodium

Paré Pointer

His poodle swallowed a clock—now he's a watchdog.

Gaucho Beef Roast

This richly glazed beef roast features a fresh Argentinean-inspired salsa that celebrates summer, and makes a pleasing change from traditional gravy.

Chopped tomato	2 cups	500 mL
Chopped fresh parsley	1 cup	250 mL
Chopped green onion	1 cup	250 mL
Olive oil	2 tbsp.	30 mL
Red wine vinegar	2 tbsp.	30 mL
Garlic cloves, minced	2	2
(or 1/2 tsp., 2 mL, powder)		
Dried oregano	1 tsp.	5 mL
Salt	1 tsp.	5 mL
Cayenne pepper	1/8 tsp.	0.5 mL
Beef top sirloin roast, trimmed of fat	4 1/2 lbs.	2 kg
Apricot jam	1/4 cup	60 mL
Chili sauce	1/4 cup	60 mL
Envelope of onion soup mix	1 1/2 oz.	42 g

Combine first 9 ingredients in medium bowl. Chill.

Place drip pan on 1 burner. To preheat barbecue, turn on burner opposite drip pan. Adjust burner to maintain interior barbecue temperature of medium. Place roast on greased grill over drip pan. Close lid. Cook for 2 hours, turning once at halftime.

Combine remaining 3 ingredients in small bowl. Brush over roast. Close lid. Cook for about 1 hour, turning once at halftime, brushing with remaining jam mixture, until internal temperature reaches 160°F (71°C) for medium or until roast reaches desired doneness. Transfer to cutting board. Cover with foil. Let stand for 10 minutes. Cut roast into slices. Serve with tomato mixture. Serves 12.

1 serving: 362 Calories; 20.1 g Total Fat (9.1 g Mono, 1.0 g Poly, 7.3 g Sat); 92 mg Cholesterol; 10 g Carbohydrate; 1 g Fibre; 34 g Protein; 751 mg Sodium

Grilled Steak and Potato Salad

A hearty meal in itself, this salad makes good use of summer vegetables. The tangy mustard dressing pairs beautifully with beef.

Olive (or cooking) oil	1/2 cup	125 mL
White wine vinegar	1/4 cup	60 mL
Dijon mustard	3 tbsp.	50 mL
Garlic cloves, minced	2	2
(or 1/2 tsp., 2 mL, powder)		
Granulated sugar	1 tsp.	5 mL
Paprika	1 tsp.	5 mL
Salt	1/2 tsp.	2 mL
Pepper	1/4 tsp.	1 mL
Beef top sirloin steak	1 lb.	454 g
Unpeeled yellow potatoes (such as Yukon Gold), cut lengthwise into 1/2 inch (12 mm) slices	1 lb.	454 g
Cut or torn romaine lettuce, lightly packed	4 cups	1 L
Chopped tomato	1 cup	250 mL
Quartered fresh white mushrooms	1 cup	250 mL

Combine first 8 ingredients in medium bowl.

Place steak in large resealable freezer bag. Pour 1/4 cup (60 mL) olive oil mixture over top. Seal bag. Turn until coated. Marinate in refrigerator for 2 hours, turning occasionally. Remove steak. Discard any remaining marinade. Preheat barbecue to medium-high. Place steak on greased grill. Close lid. Cook for about 5 minutes per side, brushing with 2 tbsp. (30 mL) olive oil mixture, until internal temperature reaches 145°F (63°C) for medium-rare or until steak reaches desired doneness. Cover with foil. Let stand for 10 minutes. Cut steak in half. Cut each half diagonally across the grain into 1/4 inch (6 mm) slices. Place in large bowl.

Place potatoes on greased grill. Close lid. Cook for about 8 minutes per side, brushing with 2 tbsp. (30 mL) olive oil mixture, until tender. Let stand until cool enough to handle. Dice. Add to steak.

Add remaining 3 ingredients and remaining olive oil mixture. Toss. Makes about 8 cups (2 L).

1 cup (250 mL): 259 Calories; 18.6 g Total Fat (11.4 g Mono, 2.1 g Poly, 4.1 g Sat); 31 mg Cholesterol; 13 g Carbohydrate; 2 g Fibre; 13 g Protein; 209 mg Sodium

Peppered Beef Skewers

Beef cubes are marinated in wine, coarsely ground pepper and pickled onions, making them succulent companions to tender-crisp grilled vegetables.

Pickled onions, rinsed and drained	8	8
Dry (or alcohol-free) red wine	1/2 cup	125 mL
Cooking oil	1 tbsp.	15 mL
Red wine vinegar	1 tbsp.	15 mL
Worcestershire sauce	1 tbsp.	15 mL
Brown sugar, packed	1 tsp.	5 mL
Coarsely ground pepper	1 tsp.	5 mL
Beef strip loin steak, cut into 16 equal pieces	1 lb.	454 g
Cherry tomatoes	16	16
Large green pepper, cut into 16 equal pieces	1	1
Small fresh white mushrooms	16	16
Bamboo skewers (8 inches, 20 cm, each), soaked in water for 10 minutes	8	8

Process first 6 ingredients in blender or food processor until finely chopped. Transfer to medium shallow bowl.

Add pepper and beef. Stir. Marinate, covered, in refrigerator for 30 minutes, stirring at halftime. Remove beef. Transfer wine mixture to small saucepan. Bring to a boil. Reduce heat to medium-low. Simmer, uncovered, for at least 5 minutes, stirring often.

Thread beef and next 3 ingredients alternately onto skewers. Preheat barbecue to medium-high. Place skewers on greased grill. Close lid. Cook, turning often, for about 10 minutes for medium-rare or until beef reaches desired doneness and vegetables are tender-crisp. Brush with wine mixture. Makes 8 skewers.

1 skewer: 128 Calories; 5.1 g Total Fat (2.3 g Mono, 0.7 g Poly, 1.4 g Sat); 25 mg Cholesterol; 5 g Carbohydrate; 1 g Fibre; 13 g Protein; 167 mg Sodium

Herb and Garlic Roast

An easy marinade made with convenient and delicious ingredients.
Marinating overnight tenderizes the roast while infusing it with subtle herb
and garlic flavours. Indirect cooking gives you time to visit with your guests!

Beef inside round roast	4 lbs.	1.8 kg
Balsamic vinaigrette dressing	1 1/2 cups	375 mL
Garlic cloves, minced	4	4
(or 1 tsp., 5 mL, powder)		
Dried basil	1 tbsp.	15 mL
Italian seasoning	1 tbsp.	15 mL
Pepper	1/2 tsp.	2 mL
Prepared beef broth	1 cup	250 mL
Chopped onion	1/2 cup	125 mL
Water	1/2 cup	125 mL

Pierce roast with large fork several times. Place in large resealable freezer bag.

Combine next 5 ingredients in medium bowl. Pour over roast. Seal bag.
Turn until coated. Marinate in refrigerator for 8 hours or overnight, turning
occasionally. Remove roast. Transfer 2/3 cup (150 mL) balsamic mixture to
drip pan. Pour remaining balsamic mixture into small saucepan. Bring to a
boil. Reduce heat to medium. Boil gently, uncovered, for at least 5 minutes,
stirring often.

Add next 3 ingredients to drip pan. Place on 1 burner. To preheat
barbecue, turn on burner opposite drip pan. Adjust burner to maintain
interior barbecue temperature of medium. Place roast on greased grill over
drip pan. Close lid. Cook for about 2 hours, turning once and brushing
with balsamic mixture, until internal temperature reaches 160°F (71°C) for
medium or until roast reaches desired doneness. Transfer to cutting board.
Cover with foil. Let stand for 10 minutes. Skim and discard fat from drip
pan. Carefully transfer drip pan mixture to blender. Carefully process until
smooth (see Safety Tip). Cut roast into slices. Serve with sauce. Serves 10.

1 serving: 374 Calories; 19.9 g Total Fat (4.4 g Mono, 0.4 g Poly, 4.9 g Sat); 114 mg Cholesterol;
7 g Carbohydrate; trace Fibre; 39 g Protein; 548 mg Sodium

Safety Tip: Follow manufacturer's instructions for processing hot liquids.

Satay Beef Ribs

Finger-lickin', tender ribs that get their rich flavour from a delicious, aromatic peanut and chili-infused sauce. Substantial and impressive!

Thai peanut sauce	1 cup	250 mL
Canned coconut milk	1/2 cup	125 mL
Finely chopped Thai hot chili peppers (see Tip, page 150), or 1/2 tsp. (2 mL) cayenne pepper	2 tsp.	10 mL
Racks of beef back ribs, bone-in (2 – 3 lbs., 900 g – 1.4 kg, each), trimmed of fat	2	2
Salt	2 tsp.	10 mL

Combine first 3 ingredients in small bowl.

Sprinkle both sides of ribs with salt. Place drip pan on 1 burner. To preheat barbecue, turn on burner opposite drip pan. Adjust burner to maintain interior barbecue temperature of medium. Place ribs, meat-side down, on greased grill over drip pan. Close lid. Cook for 1 hour. Turn. Close lid. Cook for about 1 hour, brushing occasionally with peanut sauce mixture, until meat is tender, glazed and pulling away from bones. Transfer to cutting board. Cover with foil. Let stand for 10 minutes. Cut into 1-bone portions. Makes about 14 ribs.

1 rib: 350 Calories; 31.1 g Total Fat (11.9 g Mono, 1.0 g Poly, 13.3 g Sat); 59 mg Cholesterol; 2 g Carbohydrate; 1 g Fibre; 15 g Protein; 686 mg Sodium

Pepper and Horseradish Steaks

Ready in 30 minutes

Sometimes less really is more, especially when it comes to the perfect steak. We've paired a classic peppercorn crust with a cool, creamy horseradish sauce to create a refined flavour contrast for this tender steak.

HORSERADISH SAUCE

Sour cream	1/4 cup	60 mL
Prepared horseradish	2 tbsp.	30 mL
Chopped fresh chives (or 3/4 tsp., 4 mL, dried)	1 tbsp.	15 mL
Mayonnaise	1 tbsp.	15 mL
Dijon mustard	1 tsp.	5 mL

(continued on next page)

Beef

PEPPERED STEAK

Salt	1/4 tsp.	1 mL
Coarsely ground pepper	3 tbsp.	50 mL
Beef top sirloin steak	1 lb.	454 g

Horseradish Sauce: Combine all 5 ingredients in small bowl. Makes about 1/2 cup (125 mL).

Peppered Steak: Combine salt and pepper in medium shallow dish. Press both sides of steaks into pepper mixture until coated. Discard any remaining pepper mixture. Preheat barbecue to medium-high. Place steaks on greased grill. Close lid. Cook for about 5 minutes per side until internal temperature reaches 145°F (63°C) for medium-rare or until steaks reach desired doneness. Transfer to large plate. Cover with foil. Let stand for 10 minutes. Serve with Horseradish Sauce. Serves 4.

1 serving: 250 Calories; 13.4 g Total Fat (3.3 g Mono, 0.3 g Poly, 5.2 g Sat); 72 mg Cholesterol; 4 g Carbohydrate; 1 g Fibre; 25 g Protein; 260 mg Sodium

Pub Steaks

Bring home the flavours of your favourite pub fare with this beer-infused steak. Enjoy with a cold pint of lager. Cheers!

Can of beer	12 1/2 oz.	355 mL
Cooking oil	1 tbsp.	15 mL
Dijon mustard	1 tbsp.	15 mL
Montreal steak spice	1 tbsp.	15 mL
Beef outside round steak, about 1 inch (2.5 cm) thick, cut into 4 pieces	1 1/2 lbs.	680 g

Montreal steak spice, sprinkle

Combine first 4 ingredients in small bowl.

Place steaks in large resealable freezer bag. Pour beer mixture over top. Seal bag. Turn until coated. Marinate in refrigerator for at least 6 hours or overnight, turning occasionally. Remove steaks. Discard any remaining beer mixture.

Sprinkle steaks with second amount of steak spice. Preheat barbecue to medium-high. Place steaks on greased grill. Close lid. Cook for about 5 minutes per side until internal temperature reaches 145°F (63°C) for medium-rare or until steaks reach desired doneness. Transfer to large plate. Cover with foil. Let stand for 10 minutes. Makes 4 pub steaks.

1 pub steak: 233 Calories; 7.2 g Total Fat (3.2 g Mono, 0.7 g Poly, 2.4 g Sat); 104 mg Cholesterol; 1 g Carbohydrate; 0 g Fibre; 38 g Protein; 202 mg Sodium

Spanish Steak Skewers

*Exotically spiced steak pieces are paired with onion wedges for a unique
flavour that may remind you of chorizo sausage. Serve with paprika and
cumin-flavoured mayonnaise and a full-bodied Spanish red wine.*

Olive (or cooking) oil	1 1/2 tsp.	7 mL
Ground cumin	1/2 tsp.	2 mL
Smoked sweet paprika	1/2 tsp.	2 mL
Salt	1/2 tsp.	2 mL
Pepper	1/2 tsp.	2 mL
Garlic cloves, minced	1	1
(or 1/4 tsp., 1 mL, powder)		
Beef top sirloin steak,	1 lb.	454 g
cut into 1 inch (2.5 cm) pieces		
Large red onion, quartered	1	1
Bamboo skewers (8 inches, 20 cm, each),	8	8
soaked in water for 10 minutes		

Combine first 6 ingredients in medium bowl.

Add beef. Stir until coated. Marinate, covered, in refrigerator for 30 minutes.

Peel off top 3 layers in a stack from each onion quarter. Cut each stack
lengthwise into 3 equal strips. Discard remaining onion or save for another
use. Thread onion and beef alternately onto doubled skewers (see Tip,
page 56). Preheat barbecue to medium-high. Place skewers on greased grill.
Close lid. Cook for about 4 minutes per side for medium-rare or until beef
reaches desired doneness. Makes 4 skewers.

*1 skewer: 205 Calories; 9.8 g Total Fat (4.5 g Mono, 0.6 g Poly, 3.4 g Sat); 60 mg Cholesterol;
3 g Carbohydrate; 1 g Fibre; 25 g Protein; 343 mg Sodium*

Paré Pointer

*When she found she wasn't the only pebble on the beach,
she became a little bolder.*

Beef

Grilled Surf and Turf

This classic combination of steak and shrimp is a natural candidate for the barbecue. A spicy cocktail sauce is great for dipping, and will remind you of summer even when the snow flies.

COCKTAIL SAUCE		
Ketchup	1/4 cup	60 mL
Prepared horseradish	2 tsp.	10 mL
Lemon juice	1 tsp.	5 mL
Hot pepper sauce	1/2 tsp.	2 mL
Worcestershire sauce	1/4 tsp.	1 mL
TURF		
Beef rib-eye steaks (about 4 oz., 113 g, each), about 1 inch (2.5 cm) thick	4	4
Montreal steak spice	1 tsp.	5 mL
Barbecue sauce	1/4 cup	60 mL
SURF		
Uncooked medium shrimp (peeled and deveined)	24	24
Bamboo skewers (8 inches, 20 cm, each), soaked in water for 10 minutes	4	4
Salt, sprinkle		
Pepper, sprinkle		

Cocktail Sauce: Combine all 5 ingredients in small cup. Makes about 1/3 cup (75 mL). Spoon into 4 small cups. Set aside.

Turf: Sprinkle both sides of steaks with steak spice. Preheat barbecue to medium-high. Place steaks on greased grill. Cook for 1 minute per side. Brush both sides of steaks with barbecue sauce. Close lid. Cook steaks for about 3 minutes per side until internal temperature reaches 145°F (63°C) for medium-rare or until steaks reach desired doneness. Transfer to large plate. Cover with foil. Let stand for 10 minutes.

Surf: Thread shrimp onto skewers. Sprinkle with salt and pepper. Place on greased grill. Cook for about 2 minutes per side until shrimp turn pink. Serve each Turf with 1 Surf and Cocktail Sauce. Serves 4.

1 serving: 213 Calories; 6.9 g Total Fat (2.6 g Mono, 0.6 g Poly, 2.4 g Sat); 115 mg Cholesterol; 10 g Carbohydrate; trace Fibre; 27 g Protein; 508 mg Sodium

Serves 12

Dijon Pepper Prime Rib

The rich flavours of Dijon, garlic and rosemary complement this delicious cut of meat. Superb for a special occasion, and as a bonus, you can use the meaty bones for soup the next day.

Bone-in prime rib roast	6 lbs.	2.7 kg
Garlic cloves, halved lengthwise	4	4
Dijon mustard	2/3 cup	150 mL
Steak sauce	2 tbsp.	30 mL
Cooking oil	1 tbsp.	15 mL
Coarse sea salt	1 tsp.	5 mL
Coarsely ground pepper	2 tsp.	10 mL
Dried rosemary, crushed	1 tsp.	5 mL

Cut 8 slits randomly into roast with tip of small, sharp knife. Push garlic clove half into each slit. Place drip pan filled halfway with water on 1 burner. Preheat barbecue to medium. Set up roast on rotisserie over drip pan (see Note). Close lid. Cook for about 30 minutes until starting to brown. Reduce heat to medium-low.

Combine remaining 6 ingredients in small bowl. Brush 1/3 cup (75 mL) over roast. Close lid. Cook for 30 minutes. Brush roast with remaining mustard mixture. Close lid. Cook for about 30 minutes until internal temperature reaches 160°F (71°C) for medium or until roast reaches desired doneness. Transfer to cutting board. Cover with foil. Let stand for at least 10 minutes. Remove bones. Cut roast into thin slices. Serves 12.

1 serving: 496 Calories; 39.1 g Total Fat (17.2 g Mono, 1.7 g Poly, 15.8 g Sat); 113 mg Cholesterol; 1 g Carbohydrate; trace Fibre; 33 g Protein; 489 mg Sodium

Note: Refer to your barbecue manual for instructions on rotisserie use. This roast will have to be weighted, otherwise the bones will overbalance the rotation.

66   Beef

Smoky Grilled Chicken

With its appetizing, richly coloured exterior, this chicken could get by on looks alone. But it doesn't have to—the rub gives the tender meat a lovely sweet-spicy smoked flavour without the need for wood chips or a smoker box.

Bone-in chicken breast halves (10 – 11 oz., 285 – 310 g, each)	6	6
Water	4 cups	1 L
Salt	1/3 cup	75 mL
Granulated sugar	1/4 cup	60 mL
Brown sugar, packed	3 tbsp.	50 mL
Smoked sweet paprika	4 tsp.	20 mL
Garlic powder	1 1/2 tsp.	7 mL
Onion powder	1 1/2 tsp.	7 mL
Chipotle chili powder (or 1/2 tsp., 2 mL, cayenne pepper)	1 tsp.	5 mL
Salt	1 tsp.	5 mL
Pepper	1/2 tsp.	2 mL

Place chicken in extra-large resealable freezer bag. Stir next 3 ingredients in large bowl until salt is dissolved. Pour over chicken. Seal bag. Chill for 1 1/2 hours. Remove chicken. Pat dry. Discard any remaining salt mixture.

Combine remaining 7 ingredients in small bowl. Rub over chicken. Chill, covered, in refrigerator for 2 hours. Preheat barbecue to medium-high. Place chicken on greased grill, skin-side down. Close lid. Cook for about 3 minutes per side until starting to brown. Turn burner under chicken off. Cook for about 25 minutes until internal temperature reaches 170°F (77°C). Serves 6.

1 serving: 289 Calories; 2.9 g Total Fat (0.7 g Mono, 0.7 g Poly, 0.8 g Sat); 132 mg Cholesterol; 10 g Carbohydrate; trace Fibre; 53 g Protein; 1643 mg Sodium

Pictured on page 54 and on back cover.

Paré Pointer

To make mistakes is one thing, but to practice them is another.

Grilled Citrus Chicken

Tender chicken with subtle flavours of citrus and spice. Serve with wedges of grilled lemon, lime and orange so your guests can squeeze as much or as little juice over their chicken as they'd like.

Butter, softened	1/4 cup	60 mL
Maple (or maple-flavoured) syrup	1 tbsp.	15 mL
Garlic cloves, minced	2	2
(or 1/2 tsp., 2 mL, powder)		
Finely diced fresh hot chili pepper	1 tsp.	5 mL
(see Tip, page 150)		
Grated lemon zest	1 tsp.	5 mL
Grated lime zest	1/2 tsp.	2 mL
Grated orange zest	1/2 tsp.	2 mL
Salt	1/2 tsp.	2 mL
Pepper	1/2 tsp.	2 mL
Whole chicken	4 lbs.	1.8 kg

Combine first 9 ingredients in small bowl.

Place chicken, backbone up, on cutting board. Cut down both sides of backbone with kitchen shears or sharp knife. Remove and discard backbone. Turn chicken over. Press chicken flat. Carefully loosen skin on breasts and legs but do not remove (see Tip, below). Spread about 1/4 cup (60 mL) butter mixture onto meat under skin. Rub remaining butter mixture over skin. Chill, covered, for 4 hours. Preheat barbecue to medium-high. Place chicken, skin-side up, on one side of greased grill. Turn burner under chicken to low, leaving opposite burner on medium. Close lid. Cook for 30 minutes. Carefully turn chicken over. Close lid. Cook for about 30 minutes until meat thermometer inserted into thickest part of thigh reads 180°F (82°C). Transfer to cutting board. Cover with foil. Internal temperature should rise to at least 185°F (85°C). Let stand for 10 minutes. Serves 6.

1 serving: 299 Calories; 16.2 g Total Fat (5.1 g Mono, 2.3 g Poly, 7.2 g Sat); 123 mg Cholesterol; 3 g Carbohydrate; trace Fibre; 34 g Protein; 348 mg Sodium

Pictured on page 54 and on back cover.

 tip To loosen skin of chicken or other poulty, lift edge of skin and gently slide fingers as far as possible underneath. Be careful not to tear the skin.

Avocado Lime Turkey Salad

Tender turkey, creamy avocado and crisp romaine work together nicely in this fresh and bright-tasting salad.

Cooking oil	3 tbsp.	50 mL
Lime juice	3 tbsp.	50 mL
Liquid honey	1 tbsp.	15 mL
Garlic cloves, minced	2	2
(or 1/2 tsp., 2 mL, powder)		
Cayenne pepper	1/4 tsp.	1 mL
Salt	1/2 tsp.	2 mL
Pepper	1/4 tsp.	1 mL
Turkey scaloppine	1 lb.	454 g
Diced avocado	1 1/2 cups	375 mL
Lime juice	2 tbsp.	30 mL
Salt, just a pinch		
Cherry tomatoes, halved	2 cups	500 mL
Chopped fresh chives	1 tbsp.	15 mL
(or 3/4 tsp., 4 mL, dried)		
Cut or torn romaine lettuce, lightly packed	4 cups	1 L

Combine first 7 ingredients in small bowl.

Place turkey in medium shallow dish. Pour lime juice mixture over top. Turn until coated. Marinate, covered, in refrigerator for 2 hours, turning occasionally. Remove turkey. Discard any remaining lime juice mixture. Preheat barbecue to medium. Place turkey on greased grill. Cook for about 2 minutes per side until no longer pink inside. Let stand until cool enough to handle. Cut into 1/2 inch (12 mm) pieces.

Put next 3 ingredients into large bowl. Toss.

Add turkey and remaining 3 ingredients. Toss. Makes about 10 cups (2.5 L).

1 cup (250 mL): 139 Calories; 8.2 g Total Fat (4.6 g Mono, 1.7 g Poly, 0.8 g Sat); 18 mg Cholesterol; 6 g Carbohydrate; 2 g Fibre; 12 g Protein; 147 mg Sodium

Pictured on page 54 and on back cover.

Yakitori

Plan ahead to grill these for old friends in the late afternoon of a hot summer's day. So quick, you won't miss a moment's conversation.

Mirin (Japanese sweet cooking seasoning)	1/4 cup	60 mL
Thick teriyaki basting sauce	1/4 cup	60 mL
Chili paste (sambal oelek)	1 1/2 tsp.	7 mL
Garlic powder	1/8 tsp.	0.5 mL
Boneless, skinless chicken thighs	1 lb.	454 g
Bamboo skewers (8 inches, 20 cm, each), soaked in water for 10 minutes	8	8
Sesame seeds, toasted (see Tip, page 86)	1 tsp.	5 mL

Combine first 4 ingredients in small bowl.

Place chicken between 2 sheets of plastic wrap. Pound with mallet or rolling pin until flattened. Cut in half lengthwise. Place in medium bowl. Add 1/4 cup (60 mL) mirin mixture. Turn until coated. Marinate, covered, in refrigerator for 30 minutes.

Thread chicken, accordion-style, onto skewers. Preheat barbecue to high. Place skewers on greased grill. Cook for about 2 minutes per side, brushing with remaining mirin mixture, until no longer pink inside.

Sprinkle with sesame seeds. Makes 8 skewers.

1 skewer: 114 Calories; 4.4 g Total Fat (1.6 g Mono, 1.0 g Poly, 1.2 g Sat); 37 mg Cholesterol; 5 g Carbohydrate; 0 g Fibre; 11 g Protein; 257 mg Sodium

Pictured at right.

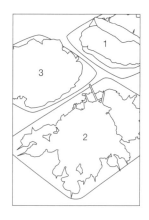

1. Chicken Souvlaki Pitas, page 38
2. Yakitori, above
3. Tropical Salmon Salad, page 96

Props: Precidio

Smoky Bacon Drumsticks

Everything's better wrapped in bacon! Especially these juicy drumsticks,
enhanced by seductive, smoky paprika.

Smoked sweet paprika	1 tbsp.	15 mL
Garlic powder	1 tsp.	5 mL
Salt	1 tsp.	5 mL
Pepper	1/2 tsp.	2 mL
Chicken drumsticks (3 – 5 oz.,	12	12
85 – 140 g, each), skin removed		
Bacon slices	12	12

Combine first 4 ingredients in small cup.

Rub paprika mixture over drumsticks. Wrap 1 bacon slice around each
drumstick. Secure with wooden picks. Preheat barbecue to medium. Place
chicken on greased grill. Close lid. Cook for about 35 minutes, turning
occasionally, until internal temperature reaches 170°F (77°C). Remove and
discard wooden picks. Makes 12 drumsticks.

1 drumstick: 108 Calories; 5.6 g Total Fat (2.3 g Mono, 1.0 g Poly, 1.7 g Sat); 42 mg Cholesterol;
trace Carbohydrate; trace Fibre; 13 g Protein; 376 mg Sodium

Pictured at left.

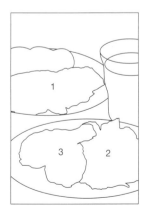

1. Ooey Gooey Chewy Panini, page 48
2. Smoky Bacon Drumsticks, above
3. Grilled Caesar Salad, page 128

Props: Stokes

⏱(30) Grilled Pineapple Chicken

Pineapple on the grill simply signals summertime. Add it to a sweet salsa that
tops spiced-up chicken and you've gone from summer to tropical vacation!
Either way, you'll feel the sun on your face and a freshness on your palate—
even if the thermometer says different!

Can of pineapple slices, drained and juice reserved	19 oz.	540 mL
Finely chopped red onion	1/4 cup	60 mL
Reserved pineapple juice	2 tbsp.	30 mL
Chopped fresh basil	1 tbsp.	15 mL
Finely grated ginger root (or 1/2 tsp., 2 mL, powder)	2 tsp.	10 mL
Liquid honey	2 tsp.	10 mL
Salt, sprinkle		
Pepper, sprinkle		
Olive oil	1 tbsp.	15 mL
Cajun seasoning	2 tsp.	10 mL
Parsley flakes	1 tsp.	5 mL
Boneless, skinless chicken thighs (about 3 oz., 85 g, each)	8	8

Preheat barbecue to medium. Place pineapple slices on greased grill. Cook for about 2 minutes per side until grill marks appear. Let stand until cool enough to handle. Chop. Transfer to small bowl.

Add next 7 ingredients. Stir.

Combine next 3 ingredients in small cup. Rub over chicken. Place chicken on greased grill. Close lid. Cook for about 7 minutes per side until internal temperature reaches 170°F (77°C). Transfer to serving plate. Serve with pineapple mixture. Serves 4.

1 serving: 377 Calories; 16.4 g Total Fat (7.4 g Mono, 3.5 g Poly, 4.1 g Sat); 112 mg Cholesterol; 26 g Carbohydrate; 2 g Fibre; 31 g Protein; 375 mg Sodium

Chicken & Turkey

Golden Beer Can Chicken

Cooking chicken on a beer can holder ensures a very moist result. This one features a slightly sweet spice coating.

Sweetened orange drink crystals	2 tbsp.	30 mL
Chili powder	1 tbsp.	15 mL
Onion powder	1 tbsp.	15 mL
Dry mustard	1 tsp.	5 mL
Garlic powder	1/2 tsp.	2 mL
Salt	1 1/2 tsp.	7 mL
Pepper	1/2 tsp.	2 mL
Whole chicken	4 lbs.	1.8 kg
Cooking oil	2 tbsp.	30 mL
Can of beer	12 1/2 oz.	355 mL

Combine first 7 ingredients in small bowl.

Sprinkle 1 tbsp. (15 mL) drink crystal mixture inside chicken cavity. Carefully loosen skin but do not remove (see Tip, page 68). Rub 3 tbsp. (50 mL) drink crystal mixture over chicken meat under skin.

Rub chicken with cooking oil. Chill, covered, for 30 minutes.

Pour 2/3 cup (150 mL) beer out of can. Reserve for another use. Slowly add remaining drink crystal mixture to can. Mixture will foam. Stand chicken, tail end down, over beer can and press down to insert can into body cavity (see Note). Put drip pan filled halfway with water on 1 burner. Preheat barbecue to medium. Place chicken upright over drip pan so that bottom of beer can rests on grill. Turn burner under drip pan to low, leaving opposite burner on medium. Close lid. Cook for about 1 hour, rotating at halftime, until browned and meat thermometer inserted in thickest part of thigh reads 180°F (82°C). Carefully remove chicken from can (see Safety Tip). Transfer to cutting board. Cover with foil. Let stand for 10 minutes. Serves 6.

1 serving: 275 Calories; 13.3 g Total Fat (5.8 g Mono, 3.3 g Poly, 2.7 g Sat); 103 mg Cholesterol; 4 g Carbohydrate; trace Fibre; 34 g Protein; 537 mg Sodium

Note: Look for inexpensive beer can chicken stands at your local department or grocery store. They are designed to hold the can and chicken safely.

Safety Tip: It is important to be very careful when removing the beer can from the chicken. The can will be full of very hot liquid.

Smoked Apple Maple Chicken

Golden chicken is subtly infused with apple and maple. Marinating makes the chicken juicy and tender.

Chicken legs, backs attached	4	4
Can of frozen concentrated apple juice, thawed	12 1/2 oz.	355 mL
Dry (or alcohol-free) white wine	3/4 cup	175 mL
Maple syrup	1/2 cup	125 mL
Soy sauce	6 tbsp.	100 mL
Garlic cloves, minced	4	4
Pepper	1 1/2 tsp.	7 mL
Maple wood chips, soaked in water for 4 hours and drained	2 cups	500 mL

Place chicken in large resealable freezer bag.

Combine next 6 ingredients in small bowl. Pour over chicken. Seal bag. Turn until coated. Marinate in refrigerator for 4 hours, turning occasionally. Remove chicken and blot dry. Transfer apple juice mixture to small saucepan. Bring to a boil. Reduce heat to medium. Boil gently, uncovered, for about 30 minutes until reduced by half. Reserve 3/4 cup (175 mL).

Put wood chips into smoker box. Place smoker box on 1 burner. Place drip pan on opposite burner. Turn on burner under smoker box to high. When smoke appears, adjust burner to maintain interior barbecue temperature of medium. Place chicken on greased grill over drip pan. Close lid. Cook for about 30 minutes per side, brushing occasionally with remaining apple juice mixture, until internal temperature reaches 170°F (77°C). Serve with reserved apple juice mixture. Serves 4.

1 serving: 467 Calories; 5.4 g Total Fat (1.6 g Mono, 1.4 g Poly, 1.4 g Sat); 104 mg Cholesterol; 68 g Carbohydrate; 1 g Fibre; 29 g Protein; 2114 mg Sodium

Chicken & Turkey

Turkish Turkey Steaks

Although turkey did not come from Turkey, the flavours popular in Turkish cooking make this healthy choice light, fresh and delicious.

Liquid honey	3 tbsp.	50 mL
Olive oil	2 tbsp.	30 mL
Garlic cloves, minced	4	4
Ground allspice	2 tsp.	10 mL
Lemon juice	1 tsp.	5 mL
Salt	1 tsp.	5 mL
Pepper	1/4 tsp.	1 mL
Boneless, skinless turkey breast steaks, halved crosswise	1 1/2 lbs.	680 g
Chopped fresh parsley	2 tbsp.	30 mL
Chopped fresh mint	1 tbsp.	15 mL
Grated lemon zest (see Tip, page 50)	1 tsp.	5 mL

Combine first 7 ingredients in small bowl.

Place turkey between 2 sheets of plastic wrap. Pound with mallet or rolling pin until an even thickness. Preheat barbecue to medium-high. Place on greased grill. Cook for 2 minutes. Turn. Brush turkey with honey mixture. Cook for 2 minutes. Turn. Brush with remaining honey mixture. Cook for about 2 minutes until no longer pink inside. Transfer to large serving platter.

Combine remaining 3 ingredients in small cup. Sprinkle over top. Serves 6.

1 serving: 207 Calories; 5.3 g Total Fat (3.3 g Mono, 0.7 g Poly, 0.7 g Sat); 45 mg Cholesterol; 11 g Carbohydrate; 1 g Fibre; 28 g Protein; 490 mg Sodium

Paré Pointer

When the butchers went on strike, things came to a grinding halt.

Curried Chicken Kabobs

A yogurt marinade makes the chicken very tender and also gives it great colour and zesty flavour. Tender-crisp veggies make these kabobs eye-catching, too.

Plain yogurt	1 cup	250 mL
Finely grated ginger root	1 tbsp.	15 mL
Paprika	1 tbsp.	15 mL
Cooking oil	2 tsp.	10 mL
Garlic cloves, minced	2	2
(or 1/2 tsp., 2 mL, powder)		
Ground cumin	1 1/2 tsp.	7 mL
Ground coriander	1 tsp.	5 mL
Salt	1 tsp.	5 mL
Turmeric	1 tsp.	5 mL
Cayenne pepper	1/4 tsp.	1 mL
Boneless, skinless chicken breast halves, cut into 1 1/2 inch (3.8 cm) pieces	1 lb.	454 g
Grape tomatoes	24	24
Large green pepper, cut into 24 pieces	1	1
Small onion, cut into 24 pieces	1	1
Bamboo skewers (8 inches, 20 cm, each), soaked in water for 10 minutes	8	8

Combine first 10 ingredients in medium bowl. Reserve 1/2 cup (125 mL) in small bowl. Chill.

Put chicken into large resealable freezer bag. Pour remaining yogurt mixture over top. Seal bag. Turn until coated. Marinate in refrigerator for 2 hours, turning occasionally. Remove chicken. Discard any remaining yogurt mixture.

Thread chicken and next 3 ingredients alternately onto skewers. Preheat barbecue to medium. Place on well-greased grill. Close lid. Cook for about 10 minutes per side, brushing with reserved yogurt mixture, until chicken is no longer pink inside. Makes 8 skewers.

1 skewer: 106 Calories; 2.2 g Total Fat (0.7 g Mono, 0.5 g Poly, 0.5 g Sat); 35 mg Cholesterol; 6 g Carbohydrate; 2 g Fibre; 15 g Protein; 260 mg Sodium

Pictured on page 53.

Rotisserie Chicken

A dinner solution that requires minimal time and effort, and produces deliciously moist and tender results! Take a chicken, add a simple rub, then skewer and truss the bird on the rotisserie and you're good to go.

Paprika	1 tbsp.	15 mL
Garlic powder	2 tsp.	10 mL
Onion powder	2 tsp.	10 mL
Pepper	2 tsp.	10 mL
Celery salt	1 tsp.	5 mL
Whole chicken	4 lbs.	1.8 kg
Cooking oil	1 tbsp.	15 mL

Combine first 5 ingredients in small cup.

Rub chicken with cooking oil. Sprinkle 1 tbsp. (15 mL) paprika mixture into cavity of chicken. Rub remaining paprika mixture over chicken. Place drip pan filled 2/3 with water on 1 burner. Preheat barbecue to medium-high. Set up chicken on rotisserie (see Note) over drip pan. Close lid. Cook for about 30 minutes until starting to brown. Reduce heat to medium. Cook for about 1 hour until meat thermometer inserted in thickest part of thigh reaches 180°F (82°C). Transfer chicken to cutting board. Cover with foil. Internal temperature should rise to at least 185°F (85°C). Let stand for 10 minutes. Serves 6.

1 serving: 251 Calories; 11.1 g Total Fat (4.4 g Mono, 2.7 g Poly, 2.6 g Sat); 103 mg Cholesterol; 2 g Carbohydrate; 1 g Fibre; 34 g Protein; 268 mg Sodium

Note: Refer to your barbecue manual for instructions on rotisserie use.

Paré Pointer

During gym class, eggs scramble up the hills.

Grilled Greek Chicken Salad

Warm grilled chicken, vegetables and toasted pita make a vibrant, rich-tasting taverna-style Greek salad perfect for a summer lunch or light dinner.

Diced Roma (plum) tomato	1 1/2 cups	375 mL
Chopped English cucumber (with peel), 1/2 inch (12 mm) pieces	1 cup	250 mL
Crumbled feta cheese	1/2 cup	125 mL
Sliced pitted kalamata olives	1/3 cup	75 mL
Balsamic vinegar	1 tbsp.	15 mL
Olive (or cooking) oil	1 tbsp.	15 mL
Slices of medium red onion, 1/2 inch (12 mm) thick	2	2
Small yellow peppers, halved	2	2
Pita bread (7 inch, 18 cm, diameter)	1	1
Olive (or cooking) oil	2 tsp.	10 mL
Greek seasoning	2 tsp.	10 mL
Boneless, skinless chicken breast halves	3/4 lb.	340 g
Olive (or cooking) oil	1 tsp.	5 mL
Greek seasoning	1 tsp.	5 mL
Cut or torn romaine lettuce, lightly packed	4 cups	1 L

Combine first 6 ingredients in large bowl.

Brush next 3 ingredients with second amount of olive oil. Sprinkle with Greek seasoning. Preheat barbecue to medium-high. Place onion, pepper and pita on greased grill. Close lid. Cook for about 4 minutes per side until grill marks appear and pita is crisp and browned. Transfer to cutting board. Let stand until cool enough to handle. Slice pepper. Chop onion. Add to tomato mixture. Stir. Break pita into bite-size pieces.

Brush chicken with third amount of olive oil. Sprinkle with second amount of Greek seasoning. Place chicken on greased grill. Close lid. Cook for about 8 minutes per side until internal temperature reaches 170°F (77°C). Transfer to cutting board. Let stand until cool enough to handle. Chop. Add chicken, pita and lettuce to tomato mixture. Toss. Makes about 10 cups (2.5 L).

1 cup (250 mL): 118 Calories; 5.5 g Total Fat (2.8 g Mono, 0.7 g Poly, 1.7 g Sat); 26 mg Cholesterol; 7 g Carbohydrate; 1 g Fibre; 10 g Protein; 181 mg Sodium

(continued on next page)

Variation: Make individual salads by arranging tomato and lettuce mixture on serving plates and topping with sliced chicken.

Pictured on page 107.

Fiesta Chicken and Salsa

Fresh and fun! Sour cream and lime make the chicken moist and tender while the crisp, colourful salsa makes a perfect contrast. The whole family will love this one.

COOL CORN SALSA

Diced avocado	1 cup	250 mL
Can of kernel corn, drained	7 oz.	199 mL
Diced English cucumber (with peel)	1/2 cup	125 mL
Diced tomato	1/2 cup	125 mL
Thinly sliced green onion	3 tbsp.	50 mL
Lime juice	1 tbsp.	15 mL
Granulated sugar	1 tsp.	5 mL
Salt	1/4 tsp.	1 mL

FIESTA CHICKEN

Sour cream	1/2 cup	125 mL
Envelope of taco seasoning mix	1 1/4 oz.	35 g
Lime juice	1 tbsp.	15 mL
Boneless, skinless chicken breast halves (4 – 6 oz., 113 – 170 g, each)	6	6

Cool Corn Salsa: Combine all 8 ingredients in medium bowl. Stir. Makes about 3 cups (750 mL). Chill.

Fiesta Chicken: Combine first 3 ingredients in small bowl. Place chicken in large resealable freezer bag. Pour sour cream mixture over top. Seal bag. Turn until coated. Marinate in refrigerator for 2 hours, turning occasionally. Remove chicken. Discard any remaining sour cream mixture. Preheat barbecue to medium. Place chicken on greased grill. Close lid. Cook for about 8 minutes per side until internal temperature reaches 170°F (77°C). Serve with Cool Corn Salsa. Serves 6.

1 serving: 255 Calories; 8.7 g Total Fat (2.8 g Mono, 0.8 g Poly, 3.3 g Sat); 79 mg Cholesterol; 12 g Carbohydrate; 2 g Fibre; 28 g Protein; 624 mg Sodium

Succulent Smoked Turkey

A great way to serve a crowd on a hot summer's day, or even a cold winter's one. Brining is the process of soaking the turkey in water and seasonings for several hours or overnight to ensure moist and well-seasoned meat all the way through. It will produce the best-tasting turkey you've ever had!

Water	8 quarts	8 L
Salt	2 cups	500 mL
Whole turkey, giblets and neck removed (not self-basting)	12 lbs.	5.4 kg
Large onion, quartered	1	1
Sprigs of fresh thyme	6	6
Sprigs of fresh sage	3	3
Cooking oil	1 tbsp.	15 mL
Onion powder	1 tbsp.	15 mL
Hickory (or mesquite) wood chips, soaked in water for 4 hours and drained	2 cups	500 mL

Stir water and salt in large stock pot or pail until salt is dissolved. Add turkey. Chill for 4 hours (see Note). Remove turkey. Discard any remaining salt mixture. Rinse turkey inside and out under running water. Drain and pat dry with paper towels. Fold wings under body.

Place next 3 ingredients in turkey cavity.

Combine cooking oil and onion powder in small bowl. Rub over turkey.

Put wood chips into smoker box. Place smoker box on 1 burner. Place drip pan filled halfway with water on opposite burner. Turn on burner under smoker box to high. When smoke appears, adjust burner to maintain interior barbecue temperature of medium. Place turkey, breast-side down, on greased grill over drip pan. Close lid. Cook for 1 hour. Carefully turn turkey over. Close lid. Cook for about 1 1/4 hours, rotating at halftime, until meat thermometer inserted in thickest part of thigh reaches 180°F (82°C). Transfer to cutting board. Cover with foil. Let stand for 20 minutes. Internal temperature should rise to at least 185°F (85°C). Remove and discard onion and herbs. Serves 12.

(continued on next page)

1 serving: 585 Calories; 29.9 g Total Fat (11.1 g Mono, 7.4 g Poly, 8.2 g Sat); 244 mg Cholesterol; trace Carbohydrate; trace Fibre; 73 g Protein; 815 mg Sodium

Note: This brine is extra salty so it does its work in short order. If you have the time and space to brine the turkey overnight, reduce the salt to 1 cup (250 mL) and follow instructions as printed.

Thai Barbecued Chicken

Are you fit to be Thai'd? Then these sweet and mildly spicy delectables will suit you fine. Use with chicken wings, if you prefer. Remember to include the long marinating time in your preparation.

Ketchup	1/2 cup	125 mL
Brown sugar, packed	3 tbsp.	50 mL
Apple cider vinegar	2 tbsp.	30 mL
Lime juice	2 tbsp.	30 mL
Soy sauce	2 tbsp.	30 mL
Fish sauce	1 tbsp.	15 mL
Chili paste (sambal oelek)	1 tsp.	5 mL
Boneless, skinless chicken thighs (about 3 oz., 85 g, each)	8	8

Combine first 7 ingredients in small bowl.

Place chicken in large resealable freezer bag. Pour ketchup mixture over top. Seal bag. Turn until coated. Marinate in refrigerator for at least 6 hours or overnight, turning occasionally. Remove chicken. Transfer ketchup mixture to small saucepan. Bring to a boil. Reduce heat to medium. Boil gently, uncovered, for at least 5 minutes until thickened and reduced by half. Preheat barbecue to medium. Place chicken on greased grill. Close lid. Cook for 12 to 14 minutes, turning occasionally and brushing with ketchup mixture, until internal temperature reaches 170°F (77°C). Makes 8 thighs.

1 thigh: 172 Calories; 6.4 g Total Fat (2.4 g Mono, 1.5 g Poly, 1.8 g Sat); 56 mg Cholesterol; 13 g Carbohydrate; trace Fibre; 16 g Protein; 680 mg Sodium

Chili-Rubbed Turkey Roll

The sweet, smoky, peppery crust of this turkey roll contrasts beautifully with the spinach-pesto filling for great flavour bite after bite. The rich colour of the crust gives this dish great eye appeal too.

Boneless, skinless turkey breast half (about 1 1/2 lbs., 680 g)	1	1
Box of frozen chopped spinach, thawed and squeezed dry	10 oz.	300 g
Fine dry bread crumbs	1/4 cup	60 mL
Sun-dried tomato pesto	1/4 cup	60 mL
Salt, sprinkle		
Brown sugar, packed	2 tbsp.	30 mL
Chili powder	2 tbsp.	30 mL
Paprika	2 tsp.	10 mL
Garlic powder	1 tsp.	5 mL
Cayenne pepper	1/4 tsp.	1 mL
Salt	1/8 tsp.	0.5 mL

To butterfly turkey, cut horizontally lengthwise, almost, but not quite through, to other side. Open flat. Place between 2 sheets of plastic wrap. Pound with mallet or rolling pin to 1/2 inch (12 mm) thickness.

Combine next 4 ingredients in small bowl. Spread evenly over turkey. Roll up tightly, jelly-roll style, starting from long edge. Tie with butcher's string.

Combine remaining 6 ingredients in small cup. Rub over turkey roll. Place drip pan filled halfway with water on 1 burner. To preheat barbecue, turn on burner opposite drip pan. Adjust burner to maintain interior barbecue temperature of medium-low. Place turkey roll on greased grill over drip pan. Close lid. Cook for about 1 1/4 hours, turning occasionally, until internal temperature of turkey (not stuffing) reaches 170°F (77°C). Transfer to cutting board. Cover with foil. Let stand for 10 minutes. Remove and discard butcher's string. Cut into 3/4 inch (2 cm) slices. Serves 6.

1 serving: 182 Calories; 1.3 g Total Fat (0.1 g Mono, 0.3 g Poly, 0.3 g Sat); 70 mg Cholesterol; 11 g Carbohydrate; 2 g Fibre; 30 g Protein; 290 mg Sodium

Pictured on page 89.

Cajun Chicken

A great-looking main course to wow your guests with, this incredibly moist chicken has wonderful Cajun flavour without the Cajun heat. The herb flavours are mild and complement the meat well. Heat lovers can up the cayenne pepper if they like.

Dried basil	1 tsp.	5 mL
Dried oregano	1 tsp.	5 mL
Paprika	1 tsp.	5 mL
Dried thyme	1/2 tsp.	2 mL
Ground cumin	1/2 tsp.	2 mL
Cayenne pepper	1/4 tsp.	1 mL
Salt	1 tsp.	5 mL
Pepper	1/4 tsp.	1 mL
Barbecue sauce	1/3 cup	75 mL
Whole chicken	4 lbs.	1.8 kg
Bay leaves	3	3
Whole black peppercorns	2 tbsp.	30 mL

Combine first 8 ingredients in small cup.

Put barbecue sauce into small bowl. Add 1 tbsp. (15 mL) basil mixture. Set aside.

Place chicken, backbone up, on cutting board. Cut down both sides of backbone with kitchen shears or sharp knife. Remove and discard backbone. Split breastbone with knife. Remove and discard. Cut skin to separate chicken halves. Rub remaining spice mixture over chicken. Chill, covered, for 30 minutes.

Fill drip pan half full of water. Add bay leaves and peppercorns. Place drip pan on 1 burner. To preheat barbecue, turn on burner opposite drip pan. Adjust burner to maintain interior barbecue temperature of medium. Place chicken, skin-side down, on greased grill over drip pan. Close lid. Cook for 20 minutes. Turn. Brush with barbecue sauce mixture. Close lid. Cook for about 50 minutes until meat thermometer inserted in thickest part of thigh reads 170°F (77°C). Transfer to cutting board. Cover with foil. Let stand for 10 minutes. Serves 6.

1 serving: 235 Calories; 9.0 g Total Fat (3.2 g Mono, 2.1 g Poly, 2.4 g Sat); 103 mg Cholesterol; 3 g Carbohydrate; 1 g Fibre; 34 g Protein; 601 mg Sodium

Five-Spice Cornish Hens

Delicate seasonings for a delicate bird. A mild Chinese five-spice flavour infuses the tasty juices, which accumulate upon standing and can be spooned over the birds for extra flavour.

Butter, softened	1/3 cup	75 mL
Sesame seeds, toasted (see Tip, below)	2 tbsp.	30 mL
Sesame oil (for flavour)	1 tbsp.	15 mL
Chinese five-spice powder	2 tsp.	10 mL
Salt	1 tsp.	5 mL
Cornish hens (about 1 1/2 lbs., 680 g, each), cleaned and trimmed	2	2

Combine first 5 ingredients in small bowl. Reserve 1 tbsp. (15 mL).

Carefully loosen skin on breasts and legs but do not remove (see Tip, page 68). Spread remaining butter mixture onto meat under skin. Spread reserved butter mixture over skin. Chill, covered, for 30 minutes. Place drip pan on 1 burner. To preheat barbecue, turn on burner opposite drip pan. Adjust burner to maintain interior barbecue temperature of medium. Place hens, breast-side down, on greased grill over drip pan. Close lid. Cook hens for 20 minutes. Turn. Close lid. Cook for about 40 minutes until meat thermometer inserted in thickest part of breast reaches 180°F (82°C). Transfer to cutting board. Cover with foil. Let stand for 10 minutes. Internal temperature should rise to at least 185°F (85°C). Cut hens in half (see Note). Serves 4.

1 serving: 616 Calories; 50.2 g Total Fat (16.8 g Mono, 6.4 g Poly, 18.2 g Sat); 251 mg Cholesterol; 2 g Carbohydrate; 0 g Fibre; 37 g Protein; 792 mg Sodium

Note: To cut Cornish hens in half, place 1 hen, breast-side down, on cutting board. Cut down both sides of backbone with kitchen shears or sharp knife to remove. Turn hen breast-side up. Cut lengthwise through breast into halves. Repeat with other hen.

 tip

When toasting nuts, seeds or coconut, cooking times will vary for each ingredient—so never toast them together. For small amounts, place ingredient in an ungreased shallow frying pan. Heat on medium for 3 to 5 minutes, stirring often, until golden. For larger amounts, spread ingredient evenly in an ungreased shallow pan. Bake in a 350°F (175°C) oven for 5 to 10 minutes, stirring or shaking often, until golden.

Chicken & Turkey

Dill Scallop Wraps

Seared lemon dill scallops, chilled vegetable-speckled rice and crispy lettuce make a light meal on a warm day.

Water	2 1/2 cups	625 mL
Arborio rice (or short-grain white rice), rinsed and drained	1 1/4 cups	300 mL
Lemon juice	2 tbsp.	30 mL
Granulated sugar	1 tbsp.	15 mL
Salt	1 tsp.	5 mL
Diced red pepper	1/3 cup	75 mL
Grated carrot	1/3 cup	75 mL
Sliced green onion	1/3 cup	75 mL
Chopped fresh dill (or 1 tsp., 5 mL, dried)	2 tbsp.	30 mL
Cooking oil	2 tbsp.	30 mL
Lemon juice	1 tbsp.	15 mL
Salt	1/2 tsp.	2 mL
Pepper	1/4 tsp.	1 mL
Large sea scallops	1 lb.	454 g
Bamboo skewers (8 inches, 20 cm, each), soaked in water for 10 minutes	8	8
Large green leaf lettuce leaves	8	8

Bring water to a boil in medium saucepan. Add rice. Stir. Reduce heat to medium-low. Simmer, covered, for 15 minutes, without stirring. Remove from heat. Let stand, covered, for about 5 minutes until rice is tender and water is absorbed. Fluff with fork. Cool.

Stir next 3 ingredients in large bowl until sugar is dissolved. Add next 4 ingredients. Stir. Add rice. Stir well. Cover. Chill.

Combine next 4 ingredients in small bowl. Thread scallops onto doubled skewers (see Tip, page 56). Brush with lemon juice mixture. Preheat barbecue to medium-high. Place on greased grill. Close lid. Cook for about 3 minutes per side until grill marks appear and scallops are opaque.

Serve scallops with rice mixture and lettuce leaves for wrapping. Makes 8 wraps.

1 wrap: 143 Calories; 4.0 g Total Fat (2.0 g Mono, 1.2 g Poly, 0.3 g Sat); 19 mg Cholesterol; 16 g Carbohydrate; 1 g Fibre; 11 g Protein; 534 mg Sodium

Cranberry Salmon on Cedar

Dried fruit and aromatic cedar combine with Asian flavours in a salmon recipe inspired by the West Coast. It's sure to impress!

Dried cranberries, chopped	2/3 cup	150 mL
Soy sauce	2 tbsp.	30 mL
Fine dry bread crumbs	3 tbsp.	50 mL
Finely chopped green onion	2 tbsp.	30 mL
Thick teriyaki basting sauce	1 tbsp.	15 mL
Salmon fillet, with skin	1 1/2 lbs.	680 g
Cedar plank, soaked in water for 1 hour	1	1

Combine cranberries and soy sauce in medium bowl. Let stand for 10 minutes until softened.

Add next 3 ingredients. Stir.

Place salmon, skin-side down, on cedar plank (see Note). Spread cranberry mixture over top. Preheat barbecue to medium-high. Reduce heat to medium-low. Place cedar plank on ungreased grill. Close lid. Cook for about 20 minutes until fish flakes easily when tested with fork. Serves 6.

1 serving: 265 Calories; 12.0 g Total Fat (5.0 g Mono, 3.2 g Poly, 3.5 g Sat); 57 mg Cholesterol; 15 g Carbohydrate; 1 g Fibre; 24 g Protein; 586 mg Sodium

Note: Cedar planks specifically designed for barbecuing can be purchased in the meat department of large grocery stores. Or use an untreated western red cedar plank from a building supply store. Never use treated cedar planks. Planks should be about 16 x 6 x 1/2 inches (40 x 15 x 1.2 cm) and are good for 1 use each.

1. Chili-Rubbed Turkey Roll, page 84
2. Sweet Stuffed Potatoes, page 121

Props: Next

Tuscan Tilapia Packets

Mild fish gets a serious flavour injection from a zesty topping of sun-dried tomato, olives and zucchini. Steaming the fish in a foil packet with vegetables keeps it nicely moist.

Diced zucchini (with peel)	1 1/2 cups	375 mL
Grated Parmesan cheese	1/2 cup	125 mL
Diced red onion	1/3 cup	75 mL
Sliced black olives, chopped	1/3 cup	75 mL
Sun-dried tomatoes in oil, blotted dry, thinly sliced	1/3 cup	75 mL
Olive oil	1 tbsp.	15 mL
Lemon juice	2 tsp.	10 mL
Italian seasoning	3/4 tsp.	4 mL
Garlic clove, minced (or 1/4 tsp., 1 mL, powder)	1	1
Salt	1/4 tsp.	1 mL
Pepper	1/4 tsp.	1 mL
Tilapia fillets (4 – 5 oz., 113 – 140 g, each), any small bones removed	4	4

Combine first 11 ingredients in medium bowl.

Cut 4 sheets of heavy-duty (or double layer of regular) foil about 14 inches (35 cm) long. Spray 1 side of each with cooking spray. Place 1 fillet in centre of each sheet. Spoon zucchini mixture over top. Fold edges of foil together over fillet to enclose. Fold ends to seal completely. Preheat barbecue to medium. Place packets, seam-side up, on ungreased grill. Close lid. Cook

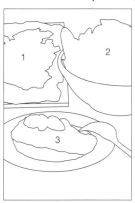

for about 15 minutes until vegetables are tender and fish flakes easily when tested with fork. Serve immediately. Serves 4.

1 serving: 246 Calories; 12.5 g Total Fat (4.7 g Mono, 1.3 g Poly, 4.5 g Sat); 72 mg Cholesterol; 6 g Carbohydrate; 2 g Fibre; 30 g Protein; 586 mg Sodium

Pictured at left.

1. Tuscan Tilapia Packets, above
2. Dark and Stormy Mussels, page 93
3. Minted Salmon, page 92

Props: Totally Bamboo
       Leonardo Da Vinci

Minted Salmon

Lemony grilled salmon is paired with a vibrant sauce of peas and fresh mint in this fresh and healthy flavour combination. Serve the sauce under the salmon to showcase the salmon's grill marks, and garnish with fresh mint sprigs.

MINTED PEA SAUCE		
Prepared chicken broth	3/4 cup	175 mL
Fresh (or frozen) peas	3/4 cup	175 mL
Chopped fresh mint	3 tbsp.	50 mL
Dijon mustard	1 tsp.	5 mL
Salt	1/8 tsp.	0.5 mL
Pepper	1/8 tsp.	0.5 mL
SPRING SALMON		
Cooking oil	1 tbsp.	15 mL
Lemon juice	2 tsp.	10 mL
Garlic powder	1/8 tsp.	0.5 mL
Salt, sprinkle		
Pepper, sprinkle		
Salmon fillets (4 – 5 oz., 113 – 140 g, each), skin and any small bones removed	4	4

Minted Pea Sauce: Pour chicken broth into medium saucepan. Bring to a boil on medium-high. Add peas. Cook, uncovered, for about 5 minutes until peas are tender. Remove from heat. Let stand for 5 minutes.

Transfer to blender. Add remaining 4 ingredients. Carefully process until smooth (see Safety Tip). Makes about 1 cup (250 mL).

Spring Salmon: Combine first 5 ingredients in small bowl. Brush on both sides of fillets. Preheat barbecue to medium-high. Place on greased grill. Close lid. Cook for about 3 minutes per side until fish flakes easily when tested with fork. Serve with Minted Pea Sauce. Serves 4.

1 serving: 266 Calories; 15.7 g Total Fat (7.1 g Mono, 4.3 g Poly, 3.9 g Sat); 57 mg Cholesterol; 6 g Carbohydrate; 2 g Fibre; 25 g Protein; 468 mg Sodium

Pictured on page 90.

Safety Tip: Follow manufacturer's instructions for processing hot liquids.

(30) Dark and Stormy Mussels

This dish is inspired by one of Bermuda's national drinks and the famous stormy waters surrounding the beautiful island. Serve with plenty of crusty bread to soak up the cooking liquid.

Fresh mussels, scrubbed clean (see Note 1)	2 lbs.	900 g
Cooking oil	2 tsp.	10 mL
Finely chopped onion	1/3 cup	75 mL
Garlic clove, minced	1	1
Ginger beer	1 cup	250 mL
Dark (navy) rum	1/4 cup	60 mL
Lime juice	1 tbsp.	15 mL
Dried crushed chilies	1/2 tsp.	2 mL
Chopped fresh parsley	2 tbsp.	30 mL

Place mussels on work surface. Lightly tap any mussels that are opened 1/4 inch (6 mm) or more. Discard any that do not close (see Note 2). Put mussels into 9 x 13 inch (22 x 33 cm) foil pan.

Heat cooking oil in medium saucepan on medium. Add onion. Cook for about 3 minutes, stirring often, until softened. Add garlic. Heat and stir for 1 minute until fragrant.

Add next 4 ingredients. Stir. Bring to a boil. Pour over mussels. Cover pan tightly with foil. Preheat barbecue to high. Place pan on ungreased grill. Close lid. Cook for about 6 minutes until mussels are opened. Discard any unopened mussels. Transfer mussels and cooking liquid to serving bowl.

Sprinkle with parsley. Serves 4.

1 serving: 137 Calories; 3.8 g Total Fat (1.7 g Mono, 1.1 g Poly, 0.4 g Sat); 17 mg Cholesterol; 10 g Carbohydrate; trace Fibre; 7 g Protein; 180 mg Sodium

Pictured on page 90.

Note 1: Remove the "beard," the stringy fibres attached to the shell, either by clipping them or giving them a sharp tug out the hinge end of the mussel (not the open end).

Note 2: It is important to discard any mussels that do not close before cooking, as well as any that have not opened during cooking.

Mirin Wasabi Tuna Skewers

Travel to Japan without leaving the backyard! Fresh tuna is marinated with sweet, salty mirin and hot wasabi, grilled on skewers and served with a spicy sauce—a delight for the taste buds!

Mirin (Japanese sweet cooking seasoning)	1/2 cup	125 mL
Sesame oil (for flavour)	2 tbsp.	30 mL
Rice vinegar	1 tbsp.	15 mL
Wasabi paste (Japanese horseradish)	1 tbsp.	15 mL
Tuna steak (about 1 inch, 2.5 cm, thick), cut into 1 inch (2.5 cm) cubes	1 1/2 lbs.	680 g
Bamboo skewers (8 inches, 20 cm, each), soaked in water for 10 minutes	6	6
Mayonnaise	2/3 cup	150 mL
Mirin (Japanese sweet cooking seasoning)	1 tbsp.	15 mL
Sesame seeds, toasted (see Tip, page 86)	1 tbsp.	15 mL
Wasabi paste (Japanese horseradish)	1 tsp.	5 mL

Whisk first 4 ingredients in large bowl until smooth. Reserve 1/4 cup (60 mL).

Add tuna to remaining mirin mixture. Stir until coated. Marinate, covered, in refrigerator for 1 hour, stirring occasionally. Remove tuna. Discard any remaining mirin mixture.

Thread tuna onto skewers. Preheat barbecue to medium-high. Place skewers on greased grill. Cook for 2 minutes, brushing with reserved mirin mixture. Turn. Cook for about 1 minute, brushing with reserved mirin mixture, until grill marks appear and tuna is medium-rare (see Note).

Combine remaining 4 ingredients in small bowl. Serve with skewers. Makes 6 skewers.

1 skewer: 372 Calories; 24.5 g Total Fat (0.2 g Mono, 0.4 g Poly, 3.5 g Sat); 62 mg Cholesterol; 6 g Carbohydrate; 0 g Fibre; 25 g Protein; 244 mg Sodium

Pictured on page 53.

Note: Tuna should always be served rare or medium-rare. Overcooked tuna becomes tasteless, tough and dry.

Stuffed Salmon

Grilling a whole fish is impressive, but stuffing it with Asian-inspired ingredients adds an extra level of flavour and elegance. Serve this dish hot or cold, with the tangy lemon mayo on the side.

Mirin (Japanese sweet cooking seasoning)	1 tbsp.	15 mL
Rice vinegar	1 tbsp.	15 mL
Granulated sugar	1 1/2 tsp.	7 mL
Salt, sprinkle		
Cooked short-grain white rice (about 1/2 cup, 125 mL, uncooked)	1 1/2 cups	375 mL
Diced zucchini (with peel)	1/2 cup	125 mL
Finely chopped red pepper	1/2 cup	125 mL
Mayonnaise	2/3 cup	150 mL
Lemon juice	2 tbsp.	30 mL
Wasabi paste (Japanese horseradish)	2 tsp.	10 mL
Grated lemon zest (see Tip, page 50)	1 tsp.	5 mL
Whole salmon, pan ready	4 lbs.	1.8 kg
Salt	2 tsp.	10 mL
Coarsely ground pepper	1 tsp.	5 mL

Stir first 4 ingredients in medium bowl until sugar is dissolved.

Add next 3 ingredients. Stir well.

Combine next 4 ingredients in small bowl. Add 2 tbsp. (30 mL) to rice mixture. Stir.

Place fish on sheet of greased heavy-duty (or double layer of regular) foil. Make 4 diagonal slashes to bone on both sides of fish. Rub salt and pepper into slashes and cavity of fish. Spoon rice mixture into cavity. Secure with metal skewers to enclose stuffing. Spread 1/3 cup (75 mL) mayonnaise mixture over top of fish and in slashes. Preheat barbecue to medium. Transfer fish, on foil, to ungreased grill. Close lid. Cook for about 45 minutes until fish flakes easily when tested with fork. Serve with remaining mayonnaise mixture. Serves 10.

1 serving: 480 Calories; 30.7 g Total Fat (8.0 g Mono, 5.1 g Poly, 7.2 g Sat); 96 mg Cholesterol; 11 g Carbohydrate; 1 g Fibre; 37 g Protein; 660 mg Sodium

Tropical Salmon Salad

Grilled salmon and mango salad is lightly dressed with a lime vinaigrette for a perfect summer meal. The marinade for the fish doubles as dressing for the salad, saving dishes and prep time.

Lime juice	1/4 cup	60 mL
Chopped fresh cilantro (or parsley)	3 tbsp.	50 mL
Cooking oil	3 tbsp.	50 mL
Liquid honey	1 tbsp.	15 mL
Grated lime zest (see Tip, page 50)	1 1/2 tsp.	7 mL
Garlic cloves, minced	2	2
(or 1/2 tsp., 2 mL, powder)		
Salt	1/2 tsp.	2 mL
Pepper	1/2 tsp.	2 mL
Dry mustard	1/4 tsp.	1 mL
Salmon fillets, skin and any small bones removed, cut into 1 inch (2.5 cm) pieces	1 lb.	454 g
Frozen mango pieces, thawed	2 cups	500 mL
Small red onion, cut into wedges and separated into layers	1/2	1/2
Bamboo skewers (8 inches, 20 cm, each), soaked in water for 10 minutes	8	8
Spring mix lettuce, lightly packed	6 cups	1.5 L

Whisk first 9 ingredients in medium bowl. Transfer 1/4 cup (60 mL) to small cup. Set aside.

Add fish to medium bowl. Stir until coated. Marinate, covered, in refrigerator for 30 minutes, stirring occasionally. Remove fish. Discard any remaining lime juice mixture.

Thread fish, mango and onion alternately onto skewers. Preheat barbecue to medium. Place skewers on greased grill. Close lid. Cook for about 4 minutes per side until fish flakes easily when tested with fork.

Remove fish, onion and mango from skewers into large bowl. Add lettuce and reserved lime juice mixture. Toss. Makes about 10 cups (2.5 L)

1 cup (250 mL): 130 Calories; 7.0 g Total Fat (3.2 g Mono, 1.9 g Poly, 1.6 g Sat); 23 mg Cholesterol; 8 g Carbohydrate; 1 g Fibre; 9 g Protein; 82 mg Sodium

Pictured on page 71.

Chipotle Shrimp Salad

A riot of colours and flavours, this salad will become a summertime favourite. With fresh mixed greens, crisp pepper, tangy tomato, smoky grilled shrimp and a citrusy dressing, it's a classic in the making.

Orange juice	1 cup	250 mL
Finely chopped chipotle peppers in adobo sauce (see Tip, page 118)	2 tsp.	10 mL
Grated orange zest (see Tip, page 50)	2 tsp.	10 mL
Granulated sugar	1 tsp.	5 mL
Salt	1 tsp.	5 mL
Pepper	1/2 tsp.	2 mL
Uncooked large shrimp (peeled and deveined)	1 lb.	454 g
Bamboo skewers (8 inches, 20 cm, each), soaked in water for 10 minutes	6	6
Cooking oil	2 tsp.	10 mL
White wine vinegar	2 tsp.	10 mL
Dijon mustard (with whole seeds)	1/2 tsp.	2 mL
Spring mix lettuce, lightly packed	6 cups	1.5 L
Thinly sliced red pepper	1 1/2 cups	375 mL
Cherry tomatoes, quartered	12	12

Whisk first 6 ingredients in small bowl. Reserve 1/3 cup (75 mL).

Thread shrimp onto skewers. Place in large shallow dish. Pour remaining orange juice mixture over top. Turn until coated. Marinate, covered, in refrigerator for 30 minutes, turning occasionally. Remove skewers. Discard any remaining orange juice mixture. Preheat barbecue to medium-high. Place skewers on greased grill. Cook for about 2 minutes per side until shrimp turn pink.

Whisk next 3 ingredients and reserved orange juice mixture in large bowl. Remove shrimp from skewers. Add to orange juice mixture.

Add remaining 3 ingredients. Toss. Makes about 10 cups (2.5 L).

1 cup (250 mL): 73 Calories; 1.9 g Total Fat (0.7 g Mono, 0.6 g Poly, 0.2 g Sat); 69 mg Cholesterol; 4 g Carbohydrate; 1 g Fibre; 10 g Protein; 194 mg Sodium

Pictured on page 126.

Citrus Pepper Halibut

Light and tender fish with citrus notes and a shot of peppery flavour. Pair with new potatoes and chilled white wine for a fresh and elegant summer dinner.

Orange juice	1/4 cup	60 mL
Lime juice	2 tbsp.	30 mL
Dried oregano	2 tsp.	10 mL
Granulated sugar	1 tsp.	5 mL
Montreal steak spice	1 tsp.	5 mL
Ground cumin	1/2 tsp.	2 mL
Halibut fillets, any small bones removed	1 lb.	454 g
Salt, sprinkle		

Combine first 6 ingredients in medium bowl.

Add fillets. Turn until coated. Marinate, covered, in refrigerator for 30 minutes, turning at half-time. Remove fillets. Transfer orange juice mixture to small saucepan. Bring to a boil. Reduce heat to medium. Boil gently, uncovered, for at least 5 minutes, stirring often. Keep warm on lowest heat.

Preheat barbecue to medium. Sprinkle both sides of fillets with salt. Place on well-greased grill. Close lid. Cook for about 4 minutes per side until fish flakes easily when tested with fork. Transfer to serving platter. Spoon orange juice mixture over top. Serves 4.

1 serving: 141 Calories; 2.8 g Total Fat (0.9 g Mono, 0.9 g Poly, 0.4 g Sat); 36 mg Cholesterol; 4 g Carbohydrate; trace Fibre; 24 g Protein; 285 mg Sodium

Dill-Crusted Tilapia

The crispy crust that surrounds this fish seals in moisture, making for crisp yet tender fillets. Simply flavoured with dill, all these need is a squeeze of lemon at serving time.

Mayonnaise	1/3 cup	75 mL
Chopped fresh dill (or 3/4 tsp., 4 mL, dried)	1 tbsp.	15 mL
Seasoned salt	1/4 tsp.	1 mL
Tilapia fillets, any small bones removed	1 lb.	454 g
Fine dry bread crumbs	1/2 cup	125 mL
Seasoned salt	1/4 tsp.	1 mL

Combine first 3 ingredients in small cup. Brush onto both sides of fillets.

(continued on next page)

Combine bread crumbs and second amount of seasoned salt in medium shallow dish. Press both sides of fillets into breadcrumb mixture until coated. Discard any remaining bread crumb mixture. Preheat barbecue to medium. Arrange fillets on large piece of greased heavy-duty (or double layer of regular) foil. Place on ungreased grill. Close lid. Cook fillets for about 5 minutes per side until fish flakes easily when tested with fork. Serves 4.

1 serving: 297 Calories; 17.3 g Total Fat (0.6 g Mono, 0.4 g Poly, 2.7 g Sat); 63 mg Cholesterol; 10 g Carbohydrate; 1 g Fibre; 25 g Protein; 439 mg Sodium

Hickory-Smoked Trout

This moist fish has an excellent smoked flavour, and is perfect chilled and used in sandwiches and salads.

Water	4 cups	1 L
Coarse (pickling) salt	1 cup	250 mL
Brown sugar, packed	1/4 cup	60 mL
Lemon juice	1/4 cup	60 mL
Chili powder	1 tsp.	5 mL
Whole rainbow trout (7 – 8 oz., 200 – 225 g, each), pan ready	2	2
Hickory wood chips, soaked in water for 1 hour and drained	2 cups	500 mL

Stir first 5 ingredients in 9 x 13 inch (22 x 33 cm) baking dish until salt is dissolved.

Place fish, backbone down, on cutting board. Cut down both sides of backbone with sharp knife or kitchen shears to, but not through, the skin. Remove and discard backbone. Press fish flat. Add to salt mixture, flesh side down. Chill, covered, for 1 hour. Remove fish. Discard salt mixture. Rinse fish. Pat dry.

Put wood chips into smoker box. Place smoker box on 1 burner. Put drip pan filled halfway with water on opposite burner. Turn on burner under smoker box to high. When smoke appears, adjust burner to maintain interior barbecue temperature of medium-low. Place fish, skin-side down, on greased grill over drip pan. Close lid. Cook for about 20 minutes until fish flakes easily when tested with fork. Let stand until cool. Chill, covered, overnight. Remove skin and bones. Makes 2 trout.

1 trout: 297 Calories; 13.1 g Total Fat (6.5 g Mono, 3.0 g Poly, 2.3 g Sat); 115 mg Cholesterol; 1 g Carbohydrate; 0 g Fibre; 41 g Protein; 1873 mg Sodium

Ready in 30 minutes Polenta and Shrimp Stacks

Look no further than this combination of creamy avocado sauce, grilled sweet peppers, crispy polenta cakes and delicate shrimp for a colourful, summery appetizer or main course. Tastes even better than it looks!

Chopped avocado	1 cup	250 mL
Mayonnaise	1/2 cup	125 mL
Lime juice	1 tbsp.	15 mL
Garlic clove, minced (or 1/4 tsp., 1 mL, powder)	1	1
Salt, sprinkle		
Pepper, sprinkle		
Tube of plain polenta (2.2 lbs., 1 kg), cut into eight 1/2 inch (12 mm) thick rounds	1/2	1/2
Grated Havarti cheese	1/2 cup	125 mL
Medium red peppers, quartered lengthwise	2	2
Uncooked medium shrimp (peeled and deveined)	32	32
Bamboo skewers (8 inches, 20 cm, each), soaked in water for 10 minutes	4	4
Olive (or cooking) oil	1 tbsp.	15 mL
Salt, sprinkle		
Pepper, sprinkle		

Process first 6 ingredients in blender or food processor until smooth. Let stand for at least 10 minutes to blend flavours.

Preheat barbecue to medium-high. Place polenta rounds on greased grill. Close lid. Cook for 3 minutes. Turn. Sprinkle with cheese. Close lid. Cook for about 3 minutes until polenta is heated through and cheese is melted. Transfer to serving plate. Cover to keep warm.

Place peppers on greased grill. Close lid. Cook for about 3 minutes per side until grill marks appear and peppers are tender.

(continued on next page)

Thread shrimp onto skewers. Brush with olive oil. Sprinkle with salt and pepper. Place on greased grill. Cook for about 2 minutes per side until shrimp turn pink. Remove shrimp from skewers. Top polenta rounds with pepper pieces, avocado mixture and shrimp, in order given. Makes 8 polenta stacks.

1 stack: 265 Calories; 21.3 g Total Fat (3.9 g Mono, 1.1 g Poly, 5.6 g Sat); 54 mg Cholesterol; 11 g Carbohydrate; 2 g Fibre; 8 g Protein; 590 mg Sodium

Lime Ginger Snapper Packets

Snapper comes out tender and delectable when you wrap it up in packets with lime, ginger, soy and cilantro and steam it on the grill. In no time, you'll have a dish with rich colour and bursts of fresh flavour.

Lime juice	2 tbsp.	30 mL
Soy sauce	2 tbsp.	30 mL
Finely grated ginger root	1 1/2 tsp.	7 mL
Sesame oil (for flavour)	1 tsp.	5 mL
Pepper	1/4 tsp.	1 mL
Snapper fillets (4 – 6 oz., 113 – 170 g, each), any small bones removed	4	4
Chopped fresh cilantro (or parsley)	1 tbsp.	15 mL
Sliced green onion	1 tbsp.	15 mL
Grated lime zest (see Tip, page 50)	1/2 tsp.	2 mL

Combine first 5 ingredients in small bowl.

Cut 4 sheets of heavy-duty (or double layer of regular) foil about 14 inches (35 cm) long. Spray 1 side with cooking spray. Place 1 fillet in centre of each sheet. Spoon lime juice mixture over top. Fold edges of foil together over fillet to enclose. Fold ends to seal completely. Preheat barbecue to medium. Place packets, seam-side up, on ungreased grill. Close lid. Cook for about 8 minutes until fish flakes easily when tested with fork. Transfer fillets and cooking liquid to serving plates.

Combine remaining 3 ingredients. Sprinkle over top. Serve immediately. Serves 4.

1 serving: 132 Calories; 2.7 g Total Fat (0.3 g Mono, 0.5 g Poly, 0.5 g Sat); 42 mg Cholesterol; 2 g Carbohydrate; trace Fibre; 24 g Protein; 731 mg Sodium

Stuffed Loin Chops

This dish looks as fantastic as it tastes! These unique pork chops are stuffed with mild sausage, cheese, apple and green onion, and are drizzled with a delectably tangy sauce.

Mild Italian sausage, casing removed	1/2 lb.	225 g
Grated Swiss cheese	1 cup	250 mL
Grated unpeeled cooking apple (such as McIntosh)	3/4 cup	175 mL
Sliced green onion	2 tbsp.	30 mL
Boneless pork loin chops (about 1 1/2 inches, 3.8 cm, thick), trimmed of fat	4	4
Frozen concentrated apple juice	2/3 cup	150 mL
Southern Comfort liqueur	2 tbsp.	30 mL
Tomato paste (see Tip, below)	2 tbsp.	30 mL
Apple cider vinegar	4 tsp.	20 mL
Brown sugar, packed	1 tbsp.	15 mL
Dried sage	1/2 tsp.	2 mL

Combine first 4 ingredients in medium bowl.

Cut horizontal slits in chops to create pockets. Fill with sausage mixture. Transfer to 9 x 9 inch (22 x 22 cm) pan.

Combine remaining 6 ingredients in small bowl. Pour over stuffed pork chops. Marinate, covered, for 2 hours. Remove pork chops. Transfer apple juice mixture to saucepan. Bring to a boil. Reduce heat to medium. Boil gently, uncovered, for at least 5 minutes, stirring often, until slightly thickened. To preheat barbecue, turn on 1 burner. Adjust burner to maintain interior barbecue temperature of medium. Arrange pork chops on greased grill over unlit burner. Close lid. Cook for about 1 hour until internal temperature of stuffing reaches 165°F (74°C). Cover with foil. Let stand for 10 minutes. Serve with sauce. Makes 4 stuffed pork chops.

1 pork chop: 478 Calories; 24.9 g Total Fat (7.3 g Mono, 1.7 g Poly, 11.0 g Sat); 94 mg Cholesterol; 28 g Carbohydrate; 1 g Fibre; 29 g Protein; 479 mg Sodium

 tip   If a recipe calls for less than an entire can of tomato paste, freeze the unopened can for 30 minutes. Open both ends and push the contents through one end. Slice off only what you need. Freeze the remaining paste in a resealable freezer bag or plastic wrap for future use.

Summer Pork Chops

Here's a recipe that combines everything we love about summer—fresh herbs, fresh vegetables and, of course, grilling! Moist, herb-infused pork chops are paired with a crisp, fresh and tangy-sweet salsa.

Finely diced tomato	1 cup	250 mL
Finely diced English cucumber (with peel)	1/2 cup	125 mL
Black olive tapenade	1/4 cup	60 mL
Chopped fresh basil	3 tbsp.	50 mL
Chopped fresh mint	1 tbsp.	15 mL
Granulated sugar	1 tsp.	5 mL
Salt	1/4 tsp.	1 mL
Pepper	1/8 tsp.	0.5 mL
Boneless pork rib chops (about 1 inch, 2.5 cm, thick), trimmed of fat (see Note)	4	4
Salt, sprinkle		
Pepper, sprinkle		
Lemon juice	2 tbsp.	30 mL
Finely chopped fresh basil	1 tsp.	5 mL

Combine first 8 ingredients in small bowl.

Sprinkle both sides of chops with second amount of salt and pepper. Preheat barbecue to medium-high. Place chops on greased grill. Close lid. Cook for about 6 minutes per side until internal temperature reaches 155°F (68°C). Transfer to serving platter. Cover with foil. Let stand for 10 minutes. Internal temperature should rise to at least 160°F (71°C).

Combine lemon juice and basil in small bowl. Brush over chops. Serve with tomato mixture. Serves 4.

1 serving: 387 Calories; 23.4 g Total Fat (9.1 g Mono, 1.7 g Poly, 7.8 g Sat); 107 mg Cholesterol; 6 g Carbohydrate; 1 g Fibre; 36 g Protein; 486 mg Sodium

Note: If boneless pork rib chops are not available, you can substitute boneless loin chops, but be sure not to overcook them as they can dry out very quickly.

Garlic Ginger Lamb Roast

Darkly caramelized, slow-roasted lamb with a glaze that's both sweet and garlicky. A superb result for not a lot of effort! Serve this tender and juicy roast with new potatoes and a green salad, or slice it up for sandwiches the next day.

Brown sugar	2/3 cup	150 mL
Soy sauce	1/2 cup	125 mL
Indonesian sweet (or thick) soy sauce	1/3 cup	75 mL
Finely grated ginger root	1 tbsp.	15 mL
Garlic cloves, minced	3	3
Cooking oil	1 tsp.	5 mL
Boneless leg of lamb roast	4 lbs.	1.8 kg

Combine first 6 ingredients in small saucepan. Heat and stir on medium-low until brown sugar is dissolved. Remove from heat. Cool.

Place roast in large resealable freezer bag. Pour soy sauce mixture over top. Seal bag. Turn until coated. Marinate in refrigerator for 4 hours, turning occasionally. Remove roast. Transfer brown sugar mixture to small saucepan. Bring to a boil on medium. Boil gently, uncovered, for about 10 minutes until thickened to syrup consistency. Place drip pan filled halfway with water on 1 burner. Preheat barbecue to medium-high. Set up roast on rotisserie over drip pan (see Note). Close lid. Cook for about 20 minutes until starting to brown. Turn off burner under roast and reduce heat on opposite side to maintain interior barbecue temperature of medium. Cook for about 1 1/2 hours, brushing occasionally with brown sugar mixture, until internal temperature reaches 160°F (71°C) for medium or until roast reaches desired doneness. Remove from rotisserie to cutting board. Cover with foil. Let stand for 10 minutes. Cut roast into thin slices. Serves 10.

1 serving: 350 Calories; 17.6 g Total Fat (7.4 g Mono, 1.3 g Poly, 6.9 g Sat); 121 mg Cholesterol; 9 g Carbohydrate; trace Fibre; 37 g Protein; 1376 mg Sodium

Note: Refer to your barbecue manual for instructions on rotisserie use.

Paré Pointer

He reminds me of a boat that honks louder when it's in a fog.

Souvlaki Morsels

These tantalizingly moist morsels of pork tenderloin are infused with the classic Greek flavours of oregano, garlic and lemon. Serve with Lemon Potato Packets, page 127, and break open a chilled bottle of retsina (Greek wine) to round out the meal.

Chopped red onion	1/2 cup	125 mL
Dry (or alcohol-free) white wine	1/4 cup	60 mL
Olive (or cooking) oil	1/4 cup	60 mL
Chopped fresh mint	2 tbsp.	30 mL
Chopped fresh oregano	2 tbsp.	30 mL
Chopped fresh parsley	2 tbsp.	30 mL
Lemon juice	1 tbsp.	15 mL
Garlic cloves, chopped	3	3
Salt	1/2 tsp.	2 mL
Coarsely ground pepper	1/2 tsp.	2 mL
Pork tenderloins, trimmed of fat (about 1 lb., 454 g, each), cut crosswise into 12 pieces	2	2
Tzatziki (optional)	1 cup	250 mL

Process first 10 ingredients in blender or food processor until almost smooth.

Place pork in large resealable freezer bag. Pour 2/3 cup (150 mL) onion mixture over top. Seal bag. Turn until coated. Marinate in refrigerator for 2 hours, turning occasionally. Remove pork. Discard any remaining onion mixture. Preheat barbecue to medium-high. Place pork on greased grill. Close lid. Cook for about 5 minutes per side, brushing with remaining onion mixture, until internal temperature reaches 155°F (68°C). Transfer to serving platter. Cover with foil. Let stand for 10 minutes. Internal temperature should rise to at least 160°F (71°C).

Serve with tzatziki if desired. Makes 12 pork morsels.

1 morsel: 140 Calories; 7.3 g Total Fat (4.5 g Mono, 1.0 g Poly, 1.6 g Sat); 49 mg Cholesterol; 1 g Carbohydrate; trace Fibre; 16 g Protein; 136 mg Sodium

Pictured on page 107.

Bacon Sage-Wrapped Pork

Impressive, yet very easy, and an economical alternative to beef tenderloin. These can be wrapped hours in advance, then grilled and served. A final sprinkling of lemon, sage and onion enhances the flavour.

Lemon juice	2 tbsp.	30 mL
Olive (or cooking) oil	1 tbsp.	15 mL
Salt	1/4 tsp.	1 mL
Pepper	1/4 tsp.	1 mL
Bacon slices	6	6
Fresh sage leaves	18	18
Boneless centre-cut pork chops (about 1 inch, 2.5 cm, thick), halved	3	3
Chopped fresh sage	1 tbsp.	15 mL
Finely chopped red onion	1 tbsp.	15 mL
Grated lemon zest (see Tip, page 50)	1 tbsp.	15 mL

Combine first 4 ingredients in small cup. Set aside.

Arrange bacon slices on work surface. Arrange 3 sage leaves along each slice. Wrap around edge of each chop, sage-side in. Secure with wooden pick. Preheat barbecue to medium-high. Brush both sides of chops with lemon juice mixture. Place on greased grill. Close lid. Cook for about 10 minutes per side until internal temperature reaches 155°F (68°C). Transfer to serving platter. Cover with foil. Let stand for 10 minutes. Internal temperature should rise to at least 160°F (71°C). Remove and discard wooden picks.

Combine remaining 3 ingredients in small bowl. Sprinkle over chops. Serves 6.

1 serving: 199 Calories; 10.3 g Total Fat (5.4 g Mono, 1.6 g Poly, 3.0 g Sat); 68 mg Cholesterol; 1 g Carbohydrate; trace Fibre; 24 g Protein; 309 mg Sodium

Pictured on page 108.

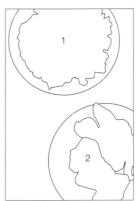

1. Grilled Greek Chicken Salad, page 80
2. Souvlaki Morsels, page 105

Whisky-Glazed Lamb Chops

*Whisky, cranberry juice and redcurrant jelly make a sweet glaze with tart
undertones. It pairs well with these succulent chops. A simple recipe with
minimal prep work for those evenings when you want to eat well with little fuss.*

Canadian whisky (rye)	1/2 cup	125 mL
Frozen concentrated cranberry juice, thawed	1/2 cup	125 mL
Redcurrant jelly	1/2 cup	125 mL
Lamb loin chops (about 1 inch, 2.5 cm, thick)	8	8
Salt, sprinkle		
Pepper, sprinkle		

Combine first 3 ingredients in small saucepan. Bring to a boil. Reduce heat
to medium-low. Simmer, uncovered, for about 12 minutes until thickened
to syrup consistency. Reserve 1/3 cup (75 mL).

Preheat barbecue to medium-high. Sprinkle both sides of chops with salt
and pepper. Brush with 1/4 cup (60 mL) remaining whisky mixture. Place
on greased grill. Close lid. Cook for about 3 minutes per side, brushing
occasionally with remaining whiskey mixture, until lamb is glazed and
internal temperature reaches 145°F (63°C) for medium-rare or until lamb
reaches desired doneness. Transfer to serving platter. Cover with foil. Let
stand for 5 minutes. Brush with reserved whisky mixture. Makes 8 chops.

*1 chop: 321 Calories; 14.8 g Total Fat (6.2 g Mono, 1.1 g Poly, 6.3 g Sat); 64 mg Cholesterol;
22 g Carbohydrate; trace Fibre; 16 g Protein; 86 mg Sodium*

1. Hazelnut-Stuffed Pork Roast, page 112
2. Parmesan Pesto Lamb, page 110
3. Bacon Sage-Wrapped Pork, page 106

Props: Moderno
        Bianco Nero

Sticky Ginger Ribs

Two kinds of ginger, one from ginger ale, give these ribs subtle flavour. The
kids will love these messy, tasty ribs for their sweet and tangy tomato sauce.

Ketchup	1 cup	250 mL
Lemon juice	3 tbsp.	50 mL
Brown sugar, packed	2 tbsp.	30 mL
Worcestershire sauce	1 tbsp.	15 mL
Dry mustard	2 tsp.	10 mL
Ground ginger	1 1/2 tsp.	7 mL
Garlic salt	1/2 tsp.	2 mL
Onion powder	1/2 tsp.	2 mL
Pepper	1/4 tsp.	1 mL
Sweet-and-sour-cut pork ribs, trimmed of fat and cut into 6-bone portions	3 lbs.	1.4 kg
Cans of ginger ale (12 1/2 oz., 355 mL, each)	2	2

Combine first 9 ingredients in medium saucepan. Bring to a boil, stirring
occasionally. Remove from heat.

Place ribs in Dutch oven. Pour ginger ale over top. Add water to cover. Bring
to a boil. Reduce heat to medium. Simmer, uncovered, for about 1 hour until
ribs are tender. Drain. Transfer to large bowl. Pour 3/4 cup (175 mL) ketchup
mixture over top. Toss until coated. Preheat barbecue to medium. Place ribs
on greased grill. Close lid. Cook for about 15 minutes, turning often and
brushing with remaining ketchup mixture, until ribs are glazed and heated
through. Cut into 3-bone portions. Makes twelve 3-bone portions.

3-bone portion: 369 Calories; 26.8 g Total Fat (11.6 g Mono, 2.4 g Poly, 10.1 g Sat);
88 mg Cholesterol; 12 g Carbohydrate; trace Fibre; 20 g Protein; 289 mg Sodium

Parmesan Pesto Lamb

Mediterranean flavours accentuate tender, delicious lamb for an easy, elegant
summer dinner. Serve with grilled peppers and zucchini and a hearty red wine.

Racks of lamb (8 ribs each)	2	2
Sun-dried tomato pesto	3 tbsp.	50 mL
Grated Parmesan cheese	1/4 cup	60 mL

(continued on next page)

Preheat barbecue to medium. Place racks, bone-side up, on greased grill. Cook for about 2 minutes until starting to brown. Transfer, bone-side down, to sheet of heavy-duty (or double layer of regular) foil.

Brush pesto over top of lamb. Sprinkle with cheese. Place racks, on foil, on ungreased grill. Close lid. Cook for about 22 minutes until internal temperature reaches 145°F (63°C) for medium-rare or until lamb reaches desired doneness. Transfer to cutting board. Cover with foil. Let stand for 10 minutes. Cut into 2-bone portions. Makes eight 2-bone portions.

2-bone portion: 230 Calories; 17.9 g Total Fat (6.8 g Mono, 1.4 g Poly, 7.8 g Sat); 65 mg Cholesterol; 1 g Carbohydrate; trace Fibre; 16 g Protein; 171 mg Sodium

Pictured on page 108.

Tangy Tomato-Mopped Pork

Pork shoulder steaks are perfect for barbecuing because they remain tender, even when cooked for longer periods of time. "Mop" them with the tangy, mustard-flavoured sauce during grilling to help keep the meat moist.

Can of tomato sauce	7 1/2 oz.	213 mL
Butter (or hard margarine)	1 tbsp.	15 mL
Dijon mustard (with whole seeds)	1 tbsp.	15 mL
Lemon juice	1 tbsp.	15 mL
Brown sugar, packed	2 tsp.	10 mL
Smoked sweet paprika	1/2 tsp.	2 mL
Smoked sweet paprika	1 tsp.	5 mL
Garlic salt	1/2 tsp.	2 mL
Pepper	1/4 tsp.	1 mL
Boneless pork shoulder butt steaks, about 3/4 inch (2 cm) thick	6	6

Combine first 6 ingredients in small saucepan. Bring to a boil, stirring occasionally. Remove from heat.

Combine next 3 ingredients in small cup. Sprinkle over both sides of steaks. Preheat barbecue to medium. Place steaks on greased grill. Close lid. Cook for about 4 minutes per side until grill marks appear. Cook for about 10 minutes, turning occasionally and brushing generously with tomato mixture, until steaks are well-done and glazed. Cover with foil. Let stand for 10 minutes. Serves 6.

1 serving: 435 Calories; 27.5 g Total Fat (11.9 g Mono, 2.3 g Poly, 10.3 g Sat); 150 mg Cholesterol; 4 g Carbohydrate; trace Fibre; 40 g Protein; 448 mg Sodium

Hazelnut-Stuffed Pork Roast

This roast is paired with a traditional stuffing enhanced with cranberry and apples.

Chopped unpeeled tart apple (such as Granny Smith)	1 cup	250 mL
Box of turkey stovetop stuffing mix, prepared according to package directions, cooled completely	4 1/4 oz.	120 g
Chopped hazelnuts (filberts), toasted (see Tip, page 86)	1/2 cup	125 mL
Chopped fresh thyme (or 1/4 tsp., 1 mL, dried)	1 tsp.	5 mL
Boneless pork loin roast (see Note)	4 lbs.	1.8 kg
Salt	1/8 tsp.	0.5 mL
Pepper	1/8 tsp.	0.5 mL
Can of jellied cranberry sauce	14 oz.	398 mL

Combine first 4 ingredients in medium bowl.

Place roast, fat-side-up, on cutting board. To butterfly roast, start horizontal cut 1/3 of the way down side of roast. Cut almost, but not quite through, to other side (see diagram 1). Turn roast over. Start second horizontal cut 1/3 of the way down side of roast. Cut almost, but not quite through, to other side (see diagram 2). Press open, fat-side down and farthest from you, to flatten (see diagram 3). Place between 2 sheets of plastic wrap. Pound with mallet or rolling pin to 1 inch (2.5 cm) thickness.

Sprinkle with salt and pepper. Spread 1 cup (250 mL) cranberry sauce on roast. Press stuffing mixture over sauce, leaving 1/2 inch (12 mm) edge. Roll up from short edge closest to you to enclose filling. Tie with butcher's string. Put drip pan filled halfway with water on 1 burner. To preheat barbecue, turn on burner under drip pan to low and burner opposite drip pan to medium. Adjust burners to maintain interior barbecue temperature of medium. Place roast, fat-side up, on greased grill over drip pan. Close lid. Cook for 1 hour. Rotate roast 180°. Brush with half of remaining cranberry sauce. Close lid. Cook for about 1 hour, brushing with remaining cranberry sauce, until browned and internal temperature of pork (not stuffing) reaches 155°F (68°C). Transfer to cutting board. Cover with foil. Let stand for 10 minutes. Internal temperature should rise to at least 160°F (71°C). Remove and discard string. Cut roast into thin slices. Serves 10.

1 serving: 423 Calories; 16.7 g Total Fat (7.0 g Mono, 1.5 g Poly, 4.2 g Sat); 100 mg Cholesterol; 25 g Carbohydrate; 2 g Fibre; 42 g Protein; 331 mg Sodium

(continued on next page)

Pictured on page 108.

Note: For best results, look for a short and wide roast as opposed to one that is long and thin.

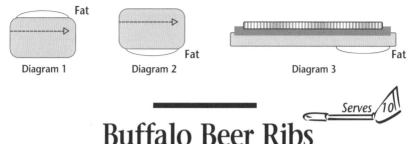

| Diagram 1 | Diagram 2 | Diagram 3 |

Buffalo Beer Ribs

Take ribs, a classic chicken wing sauce and a couple of cans of beer and you get a tender show-stopper with a spicy bite!

Pork side ribs, trimmed of fat and cut into 3-bone portions	4 lbs.	1.8 kg
Cans of beer (12 1/2 oz., 355 mL, each)	2	2
Butter (or hard margarine)	1/4 cup	60 mL
Garlic cloves, minced (or 1/2 tsp., 2 mL, powder)	2	2
Can of tomato sauce	7 1/2 oz.	213 mL
Brown sugar, packed	1/4 cup	60 mL
Louisiana hot sauce	3 tbsp.	50 mL
Apple cider vinegar	1 tbsp.	15 mL
Dried oregano	2 tsp.	10 mL
Salt	1/2 tsp.	2 mL
Pepper	1/2 tsp.	2 mL

Place ribs in Dutch oven or large pot. Pour beer over top. Add water to cover. Bring to a boil. Reduce heat to medium-low. Simmer, covered, for about 1 hour until ribs are tender. Drain.

Melt butter in medium saucepan on medium. Add garlic. Cook for about 5 minutes, stirring often, until fragrant.

Add remaining 7 ingredients. Bring to a boil. Reduce heat to low. Simmer for 10 minutes to blend flavours. Let stand for about 10 minutes until slightly cooled. Preheat barbecue to medium. Place ribs on greased grill. Close lid. Cook for about 15 minutes, turning twice and brushing with tomato mixture until ribs are glazed and heated through. Makes about ten 3-bone portions.

3-bone portion: 378 Calories; 29.2 g Total Fat (12.4 g Mono, 2.1 g Poly, 12.0 g Sat); 110 mg Cholesterol; 7 g Carbohydrate; trace Fibre; 21 g Protein; 465 mg Sodium

Pictured on front cover.

Smoky Pulled Pork

A perfect dish for a summer potluck—make it ahead or cook while visiting with your guests. Tender shreds of pork in a tangy tomato sauce make for great sandwiches. Just have your guests bring the cold beer, salads and pickles!

Garlic cloves, minced	6	6
Brown sugar, packed	1 tbsp.	15 mL
Salt	1 tbsp.	15 mL
Smoked sweet paprika	1 tbsp.	15 mL
Chili powder	2 tsp.	10 mL
Boneless pork shoulder butt roast	6 lbs.	2.7 kg
Hickory wood chips, soaked in water for 1 hour and drained	2 cups	500 mL
Apple cider vinegar	1 cup	250 mL
Ketchup	1 cup	250 mL
Brown sugar, packed	1/2 cup	125 mL
Chili sauce	1/2 cup	125 mL
Louisiana hot sauce	1 tbsp.	15 mL
Worcestershire sauce	1 tbsp.	15 mL
Salt	1 tsp.	5 mL

Stir first 5 ingredients in small bowl until mixture forms a paste. Rub over roast.

Put wood chips into smoker box. Place smoker box on 1 burner. Place drip pan filled halfway with hot water on opposite burner. Turn on burner under smoker box to high. When smoke appears, adjust burner to maintain interior barbecue temperature of high. Place roast on greased grill over drip pan. Close lid. Cook for about 4 1/2 hours, turning roast twice, until meat is fork-tender. Transfer to large bowl. Shred pork with 2 forks.

Combine remaining 7 ingredients in small saucepan. Bring to a boil. Add to pork. Stir until coated. Makes about 8 cups (2 L).

1/2 cup (125 mL): 307 Calories; 9.0 g Total Fat (4.1 g Mono, 1.0 g Poly, 3.1 g Sat); 94 mg Cholesterol; 18 g Carbohydrate; trace Fibre; 37 g Protein; 1049 mg Sodium

Sesame Mandarin Pork Salad

Turn a salad into a fabulous summer meal by adding tender bites of grilled pork that are infused with citrusy orange and rich sesame. This could also be a starter for an Asian-themed meal.

White balsamic (or white wine) vinegar	1/3 cup	75 mL
Hoisin sauce	1/4 cup	60 mL
Cooking oil	3 tbsp.	50 mL
Frozen concentrated orange juice, thawed	3 tbsp.	50 mL
Sesame oil (for flavour)	2 tbsp.	30 mL
Boneless pork loin chops, trimmed of fat	1 lb.	454 g
Mixed salad greens, lightly packed	6 cups	1.5 L
Can of mandarin orange segments, drained and juice reserved	10 oz.	284 mL
Dry chow mein noodles	1 cup	250 mL
Fresh bean sprouts	1 cup	250 mL
Sliced green onion	1/4 cup	60 mL
Reserved mandarin orange juice	3 tbsp.	50 mL

Combine first 5 ingredients in small bowl.

Pierce both sides of chops with fork several times. Place in large resealable freezer bag. Pour 1/2 cup (125 mL) marinade over top. Store remainder in fridge until ready to use. Seal bag. Turn until coated. Marinate in refrigerator for at least 6 hours or overnight, turning occasionally. Remove chops. Discard marinade. Preheat barbecue to medium-high. Place chops on greased grill. Close lid. Cook for about 5 minutes per side until internal temperature reaches 155°F (68°C). Transfer to cutting board. Cover with foil. Let stand for 10 minutes. Internal temperature should rise to at least 160°F (71°C). Slice thinly. Transfer to large bowl.

Add next 5 ingredients. Toss.

Add reserved orange juice to remaining balsamic mixture. Stir. Drizzle over pork mixture. Toss. Makes about 10 cups (2.5 L).

1 cup (250 mL): 184 Calories; 10.6 g Total Fat (3.8 g Mono, 2.0 g Poly, 2.2 g Sat); 24 mg Cholesterol; 14 g Carbohydrate; 1 g Fibre; 9 g Protein; 198 mg Sodium

Spicy Peach-Stuffed Pork Loin

Fruit and spice are always delicious with pork. For a little twist on tradition, peaches bring summery sweetness to the pork while chili paste brings heat. Lime and cilantro round it out with sour citrus and fresh herb flavour.

Chopped onion	1 cup	250 mL
Reserved peach juice	1 cup	250 mL
Soy sauce	1/4 cup	60 mL
Finely grated ginger root	3 tbsp.	50 mL
Garlic cloves, minced	4	4
Chili paste (sambal oelek)	1 tbsp.	15 mL
Boneless pork loin roast	3 1/2 lbs.	1.6 kg
Can of sliced peaches in juice, drained and juice reserved, chopped	14 oz.	398 mL
Crushed gingersnaps (about 12)	1/2 cup	125 mL
Chopped fresh cilantro (or parsley)	3 tbsp.	50 mL
Brown sugar, packed	1 tbsp.	15 mL
Chili paste (sambal oelek)	1 tbsp.	15 mL
Salt	1/2 tsp.	2 mL
Pepper	1/2 tsp.	2 mL

Process first 6 ingredients in blender or food processor until smooth.

To butterfly roast, cut horizontally lengthwise almost, but not quite through, to other side. Place roast in large resealable freezer bag. Pour onion mixture over top. Seal bag. Turn until coated. Marinate in refrigerator for at least 6 hours or overnight, turning occasionally. Remove roast. Discard onion mixture.

Combine remaining 7 ingredients in medium bowl. Open roast, fat-side down, on work surface. Press to flatten. Spoon peach mixture over roast, leaving 1/2 inch (12 mm) edge. Fold over from long edge to enclose filling. Tie with butcher's string or secure with metal skewers. Secure short ends with wooden picks. Place drip pan on 1 burner. To preheat barbecue, turn on burner opposite drip pan. Adjust burner to maintain interior barbecue temperature of medium. Place roast, fat-side up, on greased grill over drip pan. Close lid. Cook for about 1 hour until internal temperature of pork (not stuffing) reaches 155°F (68°C). Transfer to cutting board. Cover with foil. Let stand for 10 minutes. Internal temperature should rise to at least 160°F (71°C). Remove and discard string and wooden picks. Cut roast into thin slices. Serves 10.

1 serving: 300 Calories; 9.3 g Total Fat (4.3 g Mono, 1.0 g Poly, 3.1 g Sat); 87 mg Cholesterol; 17 g Carbohydrate; 1 g Fibre; 35 g Protein; 390 mg Sodium

Southern BBQ Pork Roast

Bourbon is a classic southern liquor, and its flavour comes through beautifully in the sauce that complements this pork so well. Make yourself a mint julep and lounge in your deck chair as the barbecue roasts this to tender perfection!

Cooking oil	1 tsp.	5 mL
Chopped onion	1 cup	250 mL
Garlic clove, minced	1	1
Tomato juice	1 cup	250 mL
Bourbon whiskey	1/2 cup	125 mL
Ketchup	1/2 cup	125 mL
Liquid honey	1/4 cup	60 mL
Cajun seasoning	2 tbsp.	30 mL
Worcestershire sauce	1 tbsp.	15 mL
Boneless pork loin roast	4 lbs.	1.8 kg
Cajun seasoning	1 tsp.	5 mL

Heat cooking oil in medium saucepan on medium. Add onion and garlic. Cook for about 5 minutes, stirring occasionally, until onion is softened and starting to brown.

Add next 6 ingredients. Stir. Bring to a boil. Reduce heat to medium-low. Simmer, uncovered, for 1 hour, stirring occasionally. Remove from heat. Let stand for 5 minutes. Carefully process in blender or food processor until smooth (see Safety Tip). Transfer 1 cup (250 mL) to small bowl. Set aside.

Sprinkle roast with second amount of Cajun seasoning. Place drip pan filled halfway with water on 1 burner. To preheat barbecue, turn on burner opposite drip pan. Adjust burner to maintain interior barbecue temperature of medium-low. Place roast on greased grill over drip pan. Close lid. Cook for 1 hour. Spread remaining tomato juice mixture over roast. Close lid. Cook for about 40 minutes until internal temperature reaches 155°F (68°C). Transfer to serving plate. Cover with foil. Let stand for 10 minutes. Internal temperature should rise to at least 160°F (71°C). Serve with reserved tomato juice mixture. Serves 10.

1 serving: 354 Calories; 12.7 g Total Fat (5.7 g Mono, 1.1 g Poly, 4.5 g Sat); 103 mg Cholesterol; 15 g Carbohydrate; trace Fibre; 37 g Protein; 624 mg Sodium

Safety Tip: Follow manufacturer's instructions for processing hot liquids.

Spicy Mango Pork Tenderloin

A tender cut of pork gets a lift from a sweet sauce with a spicy kick. Nice with rice or noodles, grilled vegetables and some ice-cold ales on the side.

Pork tenderloin, trimmed of fat	1 lb.	454 g
Seasoned salt	1/2 tsp.	2 mL
Roasted red peppers	1/2 cup	125 mL
Apple cider vinegar	1/4 cup	60 mL
Brown sugar, packed	1/4 cup	60 mL
Chopped onion	1/4 cup	60 mL
Frozen mango pieces, thawed	1 cup	250 mL
Garlic clove, minced	1	1
(or 1/4 tsp., 1 mL, powder)		
Finely chopped chipotle peppers in adobo sauce (see Tip, below)	1/2 tsp.	2 mL
Salt	1/4 tsp.	1 mL

Sprinkle tenderloin with seasoned salt. Chill, covered, in refrigerator for 30 minutes.

Process remaining 8 ingredients in blender or food processor until smooth. Transfer to small saucepan. Bring to a boil. Reduce heat to medium-low. Simmer, uncovered, for about 20 minutes, stirring occasionally, until thickened. Reserve 3/4 cup (175 mL). Preheat barbecue to medium. Place tenderloin on greased grill. Close lid. Cook, turning occasionally and brushing with remaining mango mixture, for about 30 minutes until internal temperature reaches 155°F (68°C). Transfer to cutting board. Cover with foil. Let stand for 10 minutes. Internal temperature should rise to at least 160°F (71°C). Cut tenderloin into thin slices. Serve with reserved mango mixture. Serves 4.

1 serving: 257 Calories; 4.0 g Total Fat (1.8 g Mono, 0.5 g Poly, 1.4 g Sat); 74 mg Cholesterol; 27 g Carbohydrate; 1 g Fibre; 25 g Protein; 677 mg Sodium

 tip   Chipotle chili peppers are smoked jalapeño peppers. Be sure to wash your hands after handling. To store any leftover chipotle peppers, divide into recipe-friendly portions and freeze, with sauce, in airtight containers for up to one year.

Apple Curry Ribs

Apple and mild curry make for a perfect combination of flavours in these succulent, fall-off-the-bone ribs. The spicy heat lingers but is mild overall, so the whole family will love them. Make sure there are plenty of napkins on hand!

Brown sugar, packed	1 tbsp.	15 mL
Garlic cloves, minced	2	2
(or 1/2 tsp., 2 mL, powder)		
Dried crushed chilies	1 tsp.	5 mL
Ground cumin	1 tsp.	5 mL
Ground ginger	1 tsp.	5 mL
Ground coriander	1/2 tsp	2 mL
Salt	1/2 tsp.	2 mL
Pepper	1/4 tsp.	1 mL
Baby back pork ribs (about 2 racks)	3 lbs.	1.4 kg
Sweetened applesauce	1 cup	250 mL
Hot curry paste	1 tbsp.	15 mL

Combine first 8 ingredients in small bowl.

Rub brown sugar mixture over ribs. Chill, covered, for 2 hours. To preheat barbecue, turn on 1 burner. Adjust burner to maintain an interior barbecue temperature of medium. Place ribs on greased grill over unlit burner. Close lid. Cook for about 1 1/4 hours, turning several times, until meat is tender and starts to pull away from bones.

Combine applesauce and curry paste in small bowl. Brush over ribs. Close lid. Cook ribs for about 30 minutes, turning several times and brushing with applesauce mixture, until meat is glazed. Transfer to large serving plate. Cover with foil. Let stand for 10 minutes. Cut into 3-bone portions. Makes about nine 3-bone portions.

3-bone portion: 462 Calories; 36.2 g Total Fat (16.1 g Mono, 3.0 g Poly, 13.3 g Sat); 122 mg Cholesterol; 8 g Carbohydrate; 1 g Fibre; 25 g Protein; 312 mg Sodium

Paré Pointer

Elbow grease is so important in the oil industry.

Skewered Italian Sausages

These tasty handmade sausages grill up golden brown and tender with a spicy-sweet flavour and notes of licorice. They pair well with new potatoes and roasted corn for a late summer lunch to remember.

Cooking oil	1/2 tsp.	2 mL
Finely chopped fennel bulb	1/4 cup	60 mL
(white part only)		
Finely chopped onion	1/4 cup	60 mL
Garlic clove, minced	1	1
(or 1/4 tsp., 1 mL, powder)		
Fine dry bread crumbs	3/4 cup	175 mL
Italian seasoning	1/2 tsp.	2 mL
Salt	1/4 tsp.	1 mL
Hot Italian sausage, casing removed	1/2 lb.	225 g
Lean ground pork	1/2 lb.	225 g
Bamboo skewers (8 inches, 20 cm, each),	8	8
soaked in water for 10 minutes		
Italian dressing	1/3 cup	75 mL

Heat cooking oil in small frying pan on medium. Add next 3 ingredients. Cook for about 5 minutes, stirring occasionally, until fennel and onion are softened. Cool. Transfer to large bowl.

Add next 3 ingredients. Stir. Add sausage and pork. Mix well.

Press about 1/3 cup (75 mL) sausage mixture around each bamboo skewer, leaving about 2 inches (5 cm) at one end. Chill, covered, for 1 hour. Preheat barbecue to medium. Place skewers on greased grill. Close lid. Cook for 10 minutes, turning often.

Brush skewers with Italian dressing. Close lid. Cook for about 5 minutes, turning once or twice and brushing with any remaining Italian dressing, until no longer pink inside. Makes 8 skewers.

1 skewer: 360 Calories; 23.3 g Total Fat (7.5 g Mono, 1.9 g Poly, 6.6 g Sat); 54 mg Cholesterol; 17 g Carbohydrate; 1 g Fibre; 19 g Protein; 918 mg Sodium

Variation: Omit Italian dressing. Brush with barbecue sauce.

Sweet Stuffed Potatoes

A pretty twist on stuffed potatoes, these can be served with grilled steak or poultry. Great for summer cooking because you don't need to turn on the oven.

Unpeeled orange-fleshed sweet potato (see Note)	1 lb.	454 g
Medium baking potatoes (about 6 oz., 170 g, each)	3	3
Herb and garlic cream cheese	1/4 cup	60 mL
Finely chopped green onion	2 tbsp.	30 mL
Sun-dried tomato pesto	2 tbsp.	30 mL
Pepper	1/8 tsp.	0.5 mL

Poke several holes randomly with fork into each sweet potato. Microwave, uncovered, on High for about 8 minutes, turning at halftime, until tender (see Tip, page 134). Wrap in tea towel. Let stand for 5 minutes. Unwrap. Let stand for about 5 minutes until cool enough to handle. Cut sweet potato in half lengthwise. Scoop out pulp into medium bowl. Discard skin. Cover pulp to keep warm.

Poke several holes randomly with fork into each potato. Microwave, uncovered, on High for about 15 minutes, turning at halftime, until tender (see Tip, page 134). Wrap in tea towel. Let stand for 5 minutes. Unwrap. Let stand for about 5 minutes until cool enough to handle. Cut potatoes in half lengthwise. Scoop out pulp, leaving 1/4 inch (6 mm) shell. Add to sweet potato. Mash.

Add remaining 4 ingredients. Stir. Spoon into shells. Preheat barbecue to medium. Place on greased warming rack of barbecue. Close lid. Cook for about 15 minutes until lightly browned and heated through. Makes 6 stuffed potatoes.

1 stuffed potato: 122 Calories; 2.4 g Total Fat (0 g Mono, trace Poly, 1.5 g Sat); 10 mg Cholesterol; 25 g Carbohydrate; 3 g Fibre; 4 g Protein; 113 mg Sodium

Pictured on page 89.

Note: These can be prepared up to a day in advance, covered, chilled, and reheated on the warming rack of the barbecue while the steaks or chicken breasts sizzle below. Increase reheat time if cooking from fridge temperature.

Herbed Cheese Biscuits

Cheese-topped buns with a surprise inside—melted cheese and delicious pesto! Easy to assemble and a great side for any barbecued meal.

Tube of refrigerator country-style biscuits (10 biscuits per tube)	12 oz.	340 g
Basil pesto	2 1/2 tsp.	12 mL
Cubes of Cheddar cheese (1/2 inch, 12 mm, pieces)	10	10
Grated Cheddar cheese	1/4 cup	60 mL

Separate biscuits. Spoon 1/4 tsp. (1 mL) pesto in centre of each biscuit. Press 1 cube of cheese into pesto. Pull sides up and pinch edges to seal. Arrange, seam-side down, in greased 9 inch (22 cm) foil pie plate.

Sprinkle with grated cheese. To preheat barbecue, turn on one burner. Adjust burner to maintain an interior barbecue temperature of medium. Place pie plate on ungreased grill over unlit burner. Close lid. Cook for about 25 minutes, rotating pan at halftime, until biscuits are browned. Let stand for 5 minutes. Makes 10 biscuits.

1 biscuit: 153 Calories; 7.2 g Total Fat (0.3 g Mono, trace Poly, 3.2 g Sat); 18 mg Cholesterol; 16 g Carbohydrate; trace Fibre; 6 g Protein; 406 mg Sodium

Pictured on page 125.

Citrus Bok Choy

If you've never tried barbecuing bok choy, well, what are you waiting for? Give it a quick grill, drizzle with sauce and—presto! —a tasty, smoky mixture of wilted-crisp greens that makes a perfect side to just about anything.

Lime juice	2 tbsp.	30 mL
Fish (or soy) sauce	1 1/2 tbsp.	25 mL
Granulated sugar	1 1/2 tbsp.	25 mL
Sesame oil (for flavour)	1 1/2 tsp.	7 mL
Chili paste (sambal oelek)	1/2 tsp.	2 mL
Whole baby bok choy, halved lengthwise	6	6

(continued on next page)

Side Dishes

Whisk first 5 ingredients in small bowl until sugar is dissolved. Reserve 2 tbsp. (30 mL).

Preheat barbecue to medium-high. Place bok choy on greased grill. Cook for about 2 minutes per side, brushing with remaining lime juice mixture, until tender-crisp. Transfer to serving plate. Drizzle with reserved lime juice mixture. Makes 12 bok choy halves.

1 bok choy half: 21 Calories; 0.6 g Total Fat (0 g Mono, 0 g Poly, 0.1 g Sat); 0 mg Cholesterol; 4 g Carbohydrate; 1 g Fibre; 1 g Protein; 209 mg Sodium

Grilled Corn Provençal

Classic Provençal flavours of garlic, tomatoes and olive oil accentuate sweet and tender grilled corn.

Butter, softened	1/4 cup	60 mL
Finely chopped onion	1/4 cup	60 mL
Finely chopped sun-dried tomatoes in oil, blotted dry	2 tbsp.	30 mL
Finely chopped fresh basil	2 tsp.	10 mL
Finely chopped fresh parsley	2 tsp.	10 mL
Finely chopped fresh thyme	2 tsp.	10 mL
White wine vinegar	2 tsp.	10 mL
Garlic cloves, minced (or 1/2 tsp., 2 mL, powder)	2	2
Salt	1/2 tsp.	2 mL
Pepper	1/2 tsp.	2 mL
Fennel seed, crushed	1/4 tsp.	1 mL
Dried crushed chilies	1/4 tsp.	1 mL
Medium corncobs, in husks	4	4

Beat first 12 ingredients in medium bowl until combined.

Pull husks down to end of cobs, leaving husks attached. Remove and discard silk. Spread butter mixture over corn. Bring husks back up to cover corn. Tie ends together with butcher's string. Preheat barbecue to medium. Place cobs on ungreased grill. Close lid. Cook for about 30 minutes, turning often, until tender. Let stand until cool enough to handle. Remove and discard husks. Makes 4 cobs.

1 cob: 207 Calories; 14.4 g Total Fat (3.3 g Mono, 0.5 g Poly, 7.3 g Sat); 30 mg Cholesterol; 19 g Carbohydrate; 3 g Fibre; 5 g Protein; 382 mg Sodium

Pictured on page 125.

Side Dishes

123

Tomato Veggie Cups

An easy, colourful side dish the whole family can enjoy. Mixed veggies in a creamy base are tucked into tomato halves and covered with melted Cheddar—what's not to love?

Frozen mixed vegetables, thawed	2 cups	500 mL
Herb and garlic cream cheese, softened	1/4 cup	60 mL
Chopped fresh dill (or 1/4 tsp., 1 mL, dried)	1 tsp.	5 mL
Medium Roma (plum) tomatoes, halved lengthwise, pulp and seeds removed	6	6
Salt, sprinkle		
Pepper, sprinkle		
Grated sharp Cheddar cheese	1/2 cup	125 mL

Combine first 3 ingredients in medium bowl.

Sprinkle inside of each tomato half with salt and pepper. Fill with vegetable mixture. Sprinkle with Cheddar cheese.

Preheat barbecue to medium. Place tomatoes on greased grill. Close lid. Cook for about 12 minutes until cheese is melted and vegetables are tender. Makes 12 tomato cups.

1 tomato cup: 57 Calories; 2.8 g Total Fat (0.5 g Mono, 0.1 g Poly, 1.8 g Sat); 10 mg Cholesterol; 6 g Carbohydrate; 1 g Fibre; 2 g Protein; 113 mg Sodium

Pictured at right.

1. Grilled Corn Provençal, page 123
2. Tomato Veggie Cups, above
3. Herbed Cheese Biscuits, page 122

Props: Ambiance

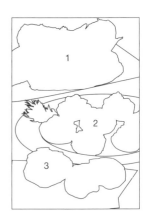

Lemon Potato Packets

A variation of a popular Greek side dish, taken outside to the barbecue and cooked in individual foil packets. Use more than one colour of potato for visual interest, and serve with other Greek-inspired dishes for a themed meal.

Baby potatoes, halved	24	24
Small red onion, cut into 12 wedges (root intact)	1	1
Garlic cloves, halved	6	6
Olive (or cooking) oil	1/3 cup	75 mL
Lemon juice	3 tbsp.	50 mL
Dried oregano	2 tsp.	10 mL
Salt	1 1/2 tsp.	7 mL
Coarsely ground pepper	1 1/2 tsp.	7 mL
Grated lemon zest (see Tip, page 50)	1 tsp.	5 mL

Cut 6 sheets of heavy-duty (or double layer of regular) foil about 12 inches (30 cm) long. Arrange potato, onion and garlic in centre of each sheet.

Combine remaining 6 ingredients in small bowl. Drizzle over potato mixture. Fold edges of foil together over potato mixture to enclose. Fold ends to seal completely. Preheat barbecue to medium. Place packets, seam-side up, on ungreased grill. Close lid. Cook for about 25 minutes, turning occasionally, until potato and onion are tender. Makes 6 packets.

1 packet: 128 Calories; 12.5 g Total Fat (8.9 g Mono, 1.8 g Poly, 1.8 g Sat); 0 mg Cholesterol; 5 g Carbohydrate; 1 g Fibre; 1 g Protein; 583 mg Sodium

Pictured at left.

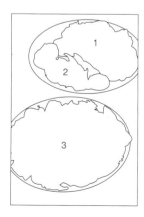

1. Bruschetta Steak Sandwiches, page 44
2. Lemon Potato Packets, above
3. Chipotle Shrimp Salad, page 97
Props: 222 Fifth

Grilled Fennel

The natural sweetness of fennel is enhanced by a short time on the grill. Brushing on a little orange juice and garlic after grilling brings out fennel's mild licorice flavour.

Orange juice	1/4 cup	60 mL
Olive (or cooking) oil	2 tbsp.	30 mL
Garlic clove, minced	1	1
(or 1/4 tsp., 1 mL, powder)		
Granulated sugar	1/2 tsp.	2 mL
Salt	1/4 tsp.	1 mL
Pepper	1/4 tsp.	1 mL
Medium fennel bulbs (white part only), halved lengthwise	2	2

Combine first 6 ingredients in small bowl.

Brush over fennel. Preheat barbecue to medium. Place fennel on greased grill. Close lid. Cook for 10 to 12 minutes per side, brushing with more orange juice mixture, until tender. Transfer to serving plate. Brush with any remaining orange juice mixture. Makes 4 fennel halves.

1 fennel half: 107 Calories; 7.3 g Total Fat (5.0 g Mono, 1.0 g Poly, 1.0 g Sat); 0 mg Cholesterol; 11 g Carbohydrate; 4 g Fibre; 2 g Protein; 206 mg Sodium

Grilled Caesar Salad

A unique spin on a classic salad! Grilling the lettuce gives it a smoky taste, but leaves it surprisingly crisp. Lots of crunchy, toasted croutons and a light, lemony dressing round out the flavours.

Cooking oil	2 tbsp.	30 mL
Lemon juice	2 tbsp.	30 mL
Coarsely ground pepper	1 tsp.	5 mL
Grated lemon zest (see Tip, page 50)	1 tsp.	5 mL
Large head of romaine lettuce, quartered lengthwise	1	1
French bread slices (1/2 inch, 12 mm, thick)	4	4

(continued on next page)

Side Dishes

Caesar dressing	1/3 cup	75 mL

Combine first 4 ingredients in small bowl.

Brush cooking oil mixture over lettuce and bread slices. Preheat barbecue to medium-high. Place bread and lettuce on greased grill. Close lid. Cook for about 3 minutes per side until bread is browned and lettuce is starting to brown. Let stand until cool enough to handle. Cut bread into 1/2 inch (12 mm) cubes. Transfer to large bowl. Chop lettuce. Add to bread.

Add dressing. Toss. Serve immediately. Makes about 8 cups (2 L).

1 cup (250 mL): 183 Calories; 10.3 g Total Fat (3.7 g Mono, 4.5 g Poly, 1.3 g Sat); trace Cholesterol; 20 g Carbohydrate; 3 g Fibre; 4 g Protein; 306 mg Sodium

Pictured on page 72.

Dressed Veggie Skewers

Grilling vegetables enhances their flavour, and the addition of bottled Italian dressing adds a complementary sweetness. The pleasing combination of shapes and colours dazzles the eye and whets the appetite.

Large red onion, quartered	1	1
Small green zucchini (with peel), cut into 8 slices (about 3/4 inch, 2 cm, thick)	2	2
Small yellow zucchini (with peel), cut into 8 slices (about 3/4 inch, 2 cm, thick)	2	2
Small fresh whole white mushrooms	24	24
Bamboo skewers (8 inches, 20 cm, each), soaked in water for 10 minutes	8	8
Italian dressing	1/2 cup	125 mL

Peel off top 3 layers in a stack from each onion quarter. Cut each stack lengthwise into 3 equal strips. Save remaining onion for another use.

Thread onion and next 3 ingredients alternately onto skewers.

Brush skewers with dressing. Preheat barbecue to high. Place skewers on greased grill. Close lid. Cook for 12 to 15 minutes, turning often and brushing with remaining dressing, until zucchini is tender. Makes 8 skewers.

1 skewer: 61 Calories; 4.2 g Total Fat (trace Mono, 0.1 g Poly, 0.5 g Sat); 0 mg Cholesterol; 5 g Carbohydrate; 1 g Fibre; 2 g Protein; 183 mg Sodium

Corny Grilled Polenta

An easy make-ahead side dish! Smoky flavour, a crisp exterior and creamy interior make this grilled polenta a perfect companion to grilled meat. Serve it with grilled vegetables as a vegetarian entree or with a dip as an appetizer.

Frozen kernel corn	1 cup	250 mL
Evaporated milk (or half-and-half cream)	1/2 cup	125 mL
Prepared chicken broth	3 cups	750 mL
Butter (or hard margarine)	1 tbsp.	15 mL
Lemon pepper	1 tsp.	5 mL
Granulated sugar	1/2 tsp.	2 mL
Yellow cornmeal	1 cup	250 mL
Grated Romano (or Parmesan) cheese	1/4 cup	60 mL
Finely chopped green onion	1 tbsp.	15 mL
Finely chopped fresh parsley	2 tsp.	10 mL
Olive (or cooking) oil	1 tbsp.	15 mL

Combine corn and milk in small microwave-safe bowl. Microwave, covered, on High for 4 minutes (see Tip, page 134). Cool slightly. Carefully process in blender until coarsely chopped (see Safety Tip). Transfer to large saucepan.

Add next 4 ingredients. Stir. Bring to a boil. Reduce heat to medium. Slowly add cornmeal, stirring constantly. Heat and stir for about 10 minutes until mixture is thick and pulls away from side of pan.

Add next 3 ingredients. Stir until cheese is melted. Spread evenly in greased 9 inch (22 cm) round cake pan. Let stand for 20 minutes. Chill for about 1 hour until set. Turn out onto cutting board. Cuts into 8 wedges (see Note).

Brush both sides of wedges with olive oil. Preheat barbecue to medium. Place polenta on well-greased grill. Close lid. Cook for about 7 minutes per side until grill marks appear and polenta is heated through. Makes 8 wedges.

1 wedge: 143 Calories; 6.1 g Total Fat (2.1 g Mono, 0.7 g Poly, 2.8 g Sat); 13 mg Cholesterol; 18 g Carbohydrate; 1 g Fibre; 5 g Protein; 884 mg Sodium

Safety Tip: Follow manufacturer's instructions for processing hot liquids.

Note: If you're not serving all the polenta right away, grill only the amount you need. Refrigerate extra triangles in an airtight container or wrapped in plastic for up to 1 week and grill as needed.

Caramelized Onion Bread

Looking for a change from garlic bread? This tasty caramelized onion bread with hints of mustard and cheese will surely do the trick!

Medium onions, cut into 1/2 inch (12 mm) slices	2	2
Bamboo skewers (8 inches, 20 cm, each), soaked in water for 10 minutes	2	2
Olive (or cooking) oil	2 tsp.	10 mL
Salt, sprinkle		
Pepper, sprinkle		
Grated Romano cheese	1/4 cup	60 mL
Dijon mustard (with whole seeds)	1 tbsp.	15 mL
Brown sugar, packed	1 tsp.	5 mL
Baguette bread loaf	1	1

Thread onion slices onto skewers. Brush with olive oil. Sprinkle with salt and pepper. Preheat barbecue to medium. Place on greased grill. Close lid. Cook for about 25 minutes, turning often, until onions are soft and golden. Remove from skewers onto cutting board. Let stand until cool enough to handle. Chop. Transfer to small bowl.

Add next 3 ingredients. Stir.

Cut loaf in half lengthwise. Spread onion mixture onto bottom half of loaf. Cover with top. Place on large sheet of greased heavy-duty (or double layer of regular) foil. Fold edges of foil together over loaf to enclose. Fold ends to seal completely. Place on ungreased grill. Close lid. Cook for about 3 minutes per side until heated through. Let stand until cool enough to handle. Remove foil. Cut into 6 portions.

1 portion: 159 Calories; 4.3 g Total Fat (1.1 g Mono, 0.2 g Poly, 1.2 g Sat); 9 mg Cholesterol; 26 g Carbohydrate; 1 g Fibre; 7 g Protein; 366 mg Sodium

Paré Pointer

Heard about the wooden rocket? Wooden nose cone, wooden cockpit, wooden fly!

Ready in 30 minutes

Pesto Vegetable Medley

A delicious variation on ratatouille that is sure to please the eye and palate. This earthy, colourful mix of grilled veggies is taken to the next level by the fresh flavour of basil pesto.

Basil pesto	1/4 cup	60 mL
Red wine vinegar	2 tbsp.	30 mL
Salt	1/4 tsp.	1 mL
Pepper	1/4 tsp.	1 mL
Sliced Asian eggplant (with peel), 1/2 inch (12 mm) thick	1 1/2 cups	375 mL
Sliced zucchini (with peel), 1/2 inch (12 mm) thick	1 1/2 cups	375 mL
Chopped red onion (1 inch, 2.5 cm, pieces)	1 cup	250 mL
Chopped red pepper (1 inch, 2.5 cm, pieces)	1 cup	250 mL
Fresh shiitake mushrooms	1 cup	250 mL

Combine first 4 ingredients in large bowl.

Add remaining 5 ingredients. Stir until coated. Cut 4 sheets heavy-duty (or double layer of regular) foil about 14 inches (35 cm) long. Spray 1 side with cooking spray. Spoon equal amounts eggplant mixture onto each sheet. Fold edges of foil together over vegetables to enclose. Fold ends to seal completely. Preheat barbecue to medium-low. Place packets, seam-side up, on greased grill. Close lid. Cook for about 15 minutes until vegetables are tender. Makes 4 packets.

1 packet: 128 Calories; 8.1 g Total Fat (trace Mono, 0.1 g Poly, 1.3 g Sat); 4 mg Cholesterol; 11 g Carbohydrate; 4 g Fibre; 4 g Protein; 288 mg Sodium

Pictured on page 18.

Paré Pointer

When his air conditioner stopped working, he just said, "A.C. come, A.C. go."

Armadillo Potatoes

Baked potatoes with a little Texas charm! Making slices across the "backs"
of these potatoes makes them look like armadillos. Parmesan and bacon add
mild but distinct flavours. Serve with sour cream if desired.

Bacon slices	4	4
Finely chopped onion	1/2 cup	125 mL
Garlic clove, minced	1	1
(or 1/4 tsp., 1 mL, powder)		
Fine dry bread crumbs	1/4 cup	60 mL
Grated Parmesan cheese	2 tbsp.	30 mL
Salt	1/8 tsp.	0.5 mL
Pepper	1/8 tsp.	0.5 mL
Medium unpeeled baking potatoes, halved lengthwise	4	4
Butter (or hard margarine), melted	1/3 cup	75 mL

Cook bacon in large frying pan on medium until crisp. Transfer with slotted spoon to paper towel-lined plate to drain. Chop finely. Drain and discard all but 1 tsp. (5 mL) drippings.

Add onion and garlic to same frying pan. Cook for about 5 minutes, stirring often, until softened. Transfer to small bowl. Let stand for about 10 minutes until cooled slightly.

Add next 4 ingredients and bacon to onion mixture. Stir.

Arrange potatoes, cut-side down, on cutting board. Cut crosswise slices into potatoes, about 1/4 inch (6 mm) apart, cutting almost, but not quite through, to flat side. Cut eight 10 inch (25 cm) squares of heavy-duty (or double layer of regular) foil. Spray with cooking spray. Place 1 potato half in centre of each square. Sprinkle bread crumb mixture over top, pressing mixture between cuts. Fold edges of foil together over potato to enclose. Fold ends to seal completely. Preheat barbecue to medium. Place packets on ungreased grill. Close lid. Cook for about 40 minutes, turning once at halftime, until potatoes are tender.

Let stand until cool enough to handle. Remove from foil. Drizzle with melted butter. Makes 8 potato halves.

1 potato half: 195 Calories; 10.3 g Total Fat (2.8 g Mono, 0.6 g Poly, 5.8 g Sat); 26 mg Cholesterol; 22 g Carbohydrate; 2 g Fibre; 5 g Protein; 231 mg Sodium

Rosemary Garlic Potato Skewers

Summer's first crop of tender baby potatoes look beautiful threaded onto skewers, and taste delicious. Garlic and rosemary offer a subtle flavour that enhances rather than dominates.

Cooking oil	1 tbsp.	15 mL
Finely chopped fresh rosemary	2 tsp.	10 mL
Garlic cloves, minced	2	2
(or 1/2 tsp., 2 mL, powder)		
Salt	1/2 tsp.	2 mL
Baby potatoes, larger ones halved	1 lb.	454 g
Bamboo skewers (8 inches, 20 cm, each), soaked in water for 10 minutes	4	4

Combine first 4 ingredients in medium bowl. Add potatoes. Toss.

Thread potatoes onto skewers (see Note). Preheat barbecue to medium. Place skewers on ungreased grill. Close lid. Cook for about 20 minutes, turning occasionally, until potatoes are golden and tender. Makes 4 skewers.

1 skewer: 126 Calories; 3.5 g Total Fat (2.0 g Mono, 1.0 g Poly, 0.3 g Sat); 0 mg Cholesterol; 21 g Carbohydrate; 1 g Fibre; 3 g Protein; 298 mg Sodium

Note: If you find it difficult to skewer the potatoes, you may want to soften them in the microwave for 1 to 2 minutes (see Tip, below).

 tip The microwaves used in our test kitchen are 900 watts—but microwaves are sold in many different powers. You should be able to find the wattage of yours by opening the door and looking for the mandatory label. If your microwave is more than 900 watts, you may need to reduce the cooking time. If it's less than 900 watts, you'll probably need to increase the cooking time.

Roasted Red Pepper Sauce

Roasted red pepper with apple overtones makes a delicious condiment for chicken or beef. You can cook the garlic and peppers at the same time. Use any leftover sauce as a spread on your next sandwich or burger.

Garlic bulb	1	1
Cooking oil	2 tsp.	10 mL
Medium red peppers, halved	6	6
Apple cider vinegar	1/4 cup	60 mL
Liquid honey	1/4 cup	60 mL
Dried basil	1 tsp.	5 mL
Fennel seed, crushed	1/2 tsp.	2 mL
Salt	1/2 tsp.	2 mL

Trim 1/4 inch (6 mm) from garlic bulb to expose tops of cloves, leaving bulb intact. Place on small sheet of greased foil. Drizzle with cooking oil. Wrap loosely in foil. Preheat barbecue to medium-high. Place packet on ungreased grill. Close lid. Cook for about 25 minutes until soft. Let stand until cool enough to handle. Squeeze garlic bulb to remove cloves from skin. Transfer to food processor. Discard skin.

Place peppers on greased grill. Close lid. Cook for about 15 minutes, turning occasionally, until skin is blistered and blackened. Transfer to large bowl. Cover with plastic wrap. Let stand for about 15 minutes until cool enough to handle. Remove and discard skins.

Add remaining 5 ingredients and red pepper to food processor. Process until smooth. Transfer to medium saucepan. Bring to a boil on medium. Boil gently, uncovered, for 8 minutes, stirring often, to blend flavours. Let stand until cool. Store in refrigerator in airtight container for up to 1 week. Makes about 2 cups (500 mL).

2 tbsp. (30 mL): 34 Calories; 0.7 g Total Fat (0.3 g Mono, 0.2 g Poly, 0.1 g Sat); 0 mg Cholesterol; 7 g Carbohydrate; 1 g Fibre; trace Protein; 71 mg Sodium

Pictured on page 144.

Tandoori Marinade

A simple marinade that tenderizes and imparts nicely balanced Indian flavours without the food colouring and MSG that so many commercial products contain. Great on chicken, pork or lamb.

Balkan-style yogurt	1 cup	250 mL
Lime juice	2 tbsp.	30 mL
Smoked sweet (or regular) paprika	2 tbsp.	30 mL
Curry powder	1 tbsp.	15 mL
Salt	1 tsp.	5 mL
Pepper	1/2 tsp.	2 mL

Combine all 6 ingredients in medium bowl. Store in refrigerator in airtight container for up to 1 week. Makes about 1 1/4 cups (300 mL).

2 tbsp. (30 mL): 16 Calories; 0.1 g Total Fat (trace Mono, trace Poly, trace Sat); 1 mg Cholesterol; 3 g Carbohydrate; trace Fibre; 2 g Protein; 256 mg Sodium

Pictured on page 143.

Steakhouse Spice Rub

A good all-purpose beef rub that may remind you of your favourite local steakhouse.

Brown sugar, packed	1 tbsp.	15 mL
Garlic powder	1 tbsp.	15 mL
Lemon pepper	1 tbsp.	15 mL
Onion powder	1 tbsp.	15 mL
Salt	1 tbsp.	15 mL
Pepper	1 tsp.	5 mL
Ground cumin	1 tsp.	5 mL
Cayenne pepper	1/2 tsp.	2 mL

Combine all 8 ingredients in small cup. Store in airtight container for up to 3 months. Makes about 1/3 cup (75 mL).

1 tsp. (5 mL): 8 Calories; 0.1 g Total Fat (0 g Mono, trace Poly, 0 g Sat); 0 mg Cholesterol; 2 g Carbohydrate; trace Fibre; trace Protein; 490 mg Sodium

Tangy and Sweet Dipping Sauce

Serve warm or cold. Tart and tangy, this sauce is great for dipping ribs and poultry or as a condiment for a pulled pork sandwich.

Chili sauce (or ketchup)	1/2 cup	125 mL
Condensed chicken broth	1/2 cup	125 mL
Frozen concentrated lemonade, thawed	1/4 cup	60 mL
Prepared mustard	1 tbsp.	15 mL
Pepper	1/4 tsp.	1 mL

Whisk all 5 ingredients in medium saucepan. Bring to a boil. Cook on medium-high, stirring occasionally, for 1 minute. Cool. Store in refrigerator in airtight container for up to 3 weeks. Makes about 1 1/4 cups (300 mL).

2 tbsp. (30 mL): 32 Calories; 0.2 g Total Fat (trace Mono, trace Poly, trace Sat); 1 mg Cholesterol; 8 g Carbohydrate; trace Fibre; trace Protein; 478 mg Sodium

Cuba Libre Marinade

Take the ingredients of a popular drink, add some oil, a little seasoning and some heat and you have a versatile marinade and glaze for beef, pork, chicken or salmon.

Can of cola beverage	12 1/2 oz.	355 mL
Dark (navy) rum	1/4 cup	60 mL
Lime juice	2 tbsp.	30 mL
Olive oil	2 tbsp.	30 mL
Seasoned salt	1/2 tsp.	2 mL
Garlic powder	1/4 tsp.	1 mL
Hot pepper sauce	1/4 tsp.	1 mL
Pepper	1/4 tsp.	1 mL

Combine all 8 ingredients in medium bowl. Store in refrigerator in airtight container for up to 1 week. Makes about 2 cups (500 mL).

2 tbsp. (30 mL): 33 Calories; 1.7 g Total Fat (1.2 g Mono, 0.2 g Poly, 0.2 g Sat); 0 mg Cholesterol; 3 g Carbohydrate; trace Fibre; trace Protein; 44 mg Sodium

Note: After meat has marinated, we recommend boiling the remaining marinade for about 30 minutes until thickened. Brush over meat while it's grilling to maximize flavour.

Mojito Butter

Fresh lime and mint-flavoured moh-HEE-toh butter with a touch of sugar and rum. This adds a burst of flavour to grilled white fish, shrimp or chicken, and it's great on corn and green beans too! The prepared butter roll may be frozen for up to one month.

Butter, softened	1/2 cup	125 mL
Finely chopped fresh mint	1 tbsp.	15 mL
Lime juice	1 tbsp.	15 mL
White (light) rum	2 tsp.	10 mL
Granulated sugar	1/2 tsp.	2 mL
Grated lime zest (see Tip, page 50)	1/2 tsp.	2 mL

Beat all 6 ingredients in small bowl until combined. Transfer to sheet of waxed paper. Form into 6 inch (15 cm) long log. Wrap in waxed paper. Chill for at least 1 hour until firm. Remove waxed paper. Cut into 1/4 inch (6 mm) slices. Makes about 24 slices.

1 slice: 35 Calories; 3.8 g Total Fat (1.0 g Mono, 0.1 g Poly, 2.4 g Sat); 10 mg Cholesterol; trace Carbohydrate; trace Fibre; trace Protein; 27 mg Sodium

Fennel Lemon Marinade

This lightly flavoured marinade is especially good with seafood or poultry.

Dry (or alcohol-free) white wine	1/2 cup	125 mL
Chopped fresh dill	2 tbsp.	30 mL
(or 1 1/2 tsp., 7 mL, dried)		
Olive (or cooking) oil	2 tbsp.	30 mL
Fennel seed, crushed	1 tbsp.	15 mL
Grated lemon zest	1 tbsp.	15 mL
Salt	1/4 tsp.	1 mL

Combine all 6 ingredients in medium bowl. Store in refrigerator in airtight container for up to 1 week. Makes about 3/4 cup (175 mL).

2 tbsp. (30 mL): 63 Calories; 5.0 g Total Fat (3.6 g Mono, 0.7 g Poly, 0.7 g Sat); 0 mg Cholesterol; 1 g Carbohydrate; 1 g Fibre; trace Protein; 103 mg Sodium

Chimichurri Aioli

Creamy garlic aioli is jazzed up with chimichurri, the classic Argentinean herb sauce. This versatile sauce is wonderful on baked potatoes, grilled vegetables, beef, burger buns, crostini, seafood and as a dip on the table for miscellaneous barbecued bits!

Egg yolks (large), see Safety Tip	3	3
Lemon juice	2 tbsp.	30 mL
Dijon mustard	1 tsp.	5 mL
Olive oil	3/4 cup	175 mL
Chopped fresh parsley	3/4 cup	175 mL
Chopped fresh cilantro	1/4 cup	60 mL
Chopped fresh oregano	1/4 cup	60 mL
Finely chopped onion	1/4 cup	60 mL
Garlic cloves, minced	3	3
Red wine vinegar	2 tsp.	10 mL
Dried crushed chilies	1/2 tsp.	2 mL
Salt	1/2 tsp.	2 mL
Pepper	1/2 tsp.	2 mL

Process first 3 ingredients in blender or food processor until combined. With motor running, add olive oil in thin stream through hole in lid until thickened.

Add remaining 9 ingredients. Process, scraping down sides if necessary, until smooth. Makes about 1 2/3 cups (400 mL).

2 tbsp. (30 mL): 126 Calories; 13.7 g Total Fat (9.5 g Mono, 2.0 g Poly, 2.2 g Sat); 46 mg Cholesterol; 1 g Carbohydrate; trace Fibre; 1 g Protein; 96 mg Sodium

Pictured on page 144.

Safety Tip: This recipe contains uncooked egg. Make sure to use fresh, clean Grade A eggs that are free of cracks. Keep chilled and consume the same day it is prepared. Always discard leftovers. Pregnant women, young children or the elderly are not advised to eat anything containing raw egg.

(15) Southern Crunch Poultry Rub

Get fried chicken flavour from the barbecue! A zesty rub that's great on chicken thighs, breasts or drumsticks.

Garlic powder	1 tbsp.	15 mL
Onion powder	1 tbsp.	15 mL
Yellow cornmeal	1 tbsp.	15 mL
Dried thyme	2 tsp.	10 mL
Dry mustard	2 tsp.	10 mL
Cayenne pepper	1 tsp.	5 mL
Celery salt	1 tsp.	5 mL
Salt	1 tsp.	5 mL
Pepper	1 tsp.	5 mL

Combine all 9 ingredients in small bowl. Store in airtight container for up to 3 months. Makes about 1/3 cup (75 mL).

1 tsp. (5 mL): 6 Calories; 0.1 g Total Fat (trace Mono, trace Poly, trace Sat); 0 mg Cholesterol; 1 g Carbohydrate; trace Fibre; trace Protein; 229 mg Sodium

Java Mop Sauce

Perfect for brushing (or mopping) onto a slowly smoking beef brisket partway through the cooking, this mop sauce is deep in colour and flavour. Use with or without a rub or barbecue sauce on any beef cooked over indirect heat.

Hot strong prepared coffee	1 cup	250 mL
Chili sauce	1/2 cup	125 mL
Ketchup	1/2 cup	125 mL
White vinegar	1/2 cup	125 mL
Butter (or hard margarine)	1/4 cup	60 mL
Worcestershire sauce	1 tbsp.	15 mL
Dried crushed chilies	1/4 tsp.	1 mL

Combine all 7 ingredients in medium saucepan. Heat and stir on medium until butter is melted. Reduce heat to medium-low. Simmer, uncovered, for about 1 hour, stirring occasionally, until reduced and thickened. Cool. Store in refrigerator in airtight container for up to 3 weeks. Makes about 1 3/4 cups (425 mL).

2 tbsp. (30 mL): 55 Calories; 3.2 g Total Fat (0.8 g Mono, 0.1 g Poly, 2.0 g Sat); 9 mg Cholesterol; 7 g Carbohydrate; trace Fibre; trace Protein; 368 mg Sodium

Pork Rub

A rub that balances earthy, robust flavours with spicy heat. Well suited to pork, especially tenderloin, steaks or chops.

Brown sugar, packed	1 tbsp.	15 mL
Garlic powder	1 tbsp.	15 mL
Onion powder	1 tbsp.	15 mL
Coarse salt	1 tbsp.	15 mL
Pepper	2 tsp.	10 mL
Smoked sweet paprika	2 tsp.	10 mL
Caraway seed	1 tsp.	5 mL
Cumin seed	1 tsp.	5 mL
Dried crushed chilies	1 tsp.	5 mL

Combine all 9 ingredients in small bowl. Store in airtight container for up to 3 months. Makes about 1/3 cup (75 mL).

1 tsp. (5 mL): 9 Calories; 0.1 g Total Fat (trace Mono, trace Poly, trace Sat); 0 mg Cholesterol; 2 g Carbohydrate; trace Fibre; trace Protein; 466 mg Sodium

Fish and Seafood Rub

This tasty rub can be used to enhance the delicate flavour of your favourite fish or seafood. Lightly spicy, it's particularly good on shrimp and haddock.

Garlic powder	1 tbsp.	15 mL
Lemon pepper	1 tbsp.	15 mL
Ground coriander	2 tsp.	10 mL
Dried basil	1 tsp.	5 mL
Dried dillweed	1 tsp.	5 mL
Cayenne pepper	1/2 tsp.	2 mL
Salt	1/2 tsp.	2 mL

Combine all 7 ingredients in small bowl. Store in airtight container for up to 3 months. Makes about 1/4 cup (60 mL).

1 tsp. (5 mL): 5 Calories; 0.1 g Total Fat (trace Mono, trace Poly, 0 g Sat); 0 mg Cholesterol; 1 g Carbohydrate; trace Fibre; trace Protein; 127 mg Sodium

Pictured on page 143.

Jamaican Jerk Paste

Traditionally used in Jamaica on pork or chicken, spicy jerk seasonings are also delicious mixed into ground lamb. The more paste you use and the longer you let it stand on the meat before you grill it, the hotter it will be!

Chopped green onion	1/2 cup	125 mL
Chopped onion	1/2 cup	125 mL
Finely chopped fresh hot chili pepper (see Tip, page 150)	1/3 cup	75 mL
Finely grated ginger root	2 tbsp.	30 mL
Lime juice	2 tbsp.	30 mL
Brown sugar, packed	1 tbsp.	15 mL
Dried thyme	1 tbsp.	15 mL
Garlic cloves, minced (or 1/2 tsp., 2 mL, powder)	2	2
Ground allspice	1 tsp.	5 mL
Salt	2 tsp.	10 mL
Pepper	1 tsp.	5 mL
Ground cinnamon	1/2 tsp.	2 mL
Ground nutmeg	1/2 tsp.	2 mL

Process first 4 ingredients in food processor until finely chopped.

Add remaining 9 ingredients. Process until smooth. Store in refrigerator in airtight container for up to 2 weeks. Makes about 1 cup (250 mL).

2 tsp. (10 mL): 8 Calories; 0.1 g Total Fat (0 g Mono, trace Poly, trace Sat); 0 mg Cholesterol; 2 g Carbohydrate; trace Fibre; trace Protein; 187 mg Sodium

Pictured at right.

1. Fish and Seafood Rub, page 141
2. Jamaican Jerk Paste, above
3. Tandoori Marinade, page 136

Props: MIKASA

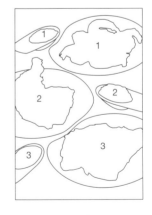

Melon Ginger Salsa

Ready in 30 minutes

Grilled melon and tomato add smoky notes to this fresh, colourful salsa while ginger beer adds spiciness and bright ginger flavour. A great side or topping for grilled meats or fish, this salsa is at its best the day it is made. Choose melons and tomatoes that are firm but ripe.

Ginger beer	1/4 cup	60 mL
Chopped fresh cilantro (or parsley)	2 tbsp.	30 mL
Finely chopped red onion	2 tbsp.	30 mL
Lemon juice	2 tbsp.	30 mL
Finely grated ginger root	2 tsp.	10 mL
Salt	1/2 tsp.	2 mL
Coarsely ground pepper	1 tsp.	5 mL
Cantaloupe wedges (with peel), 1/2 inch (12 mm) thick	5	5
Honeydew wedges (with peel), 1/2 inch (12 mm) thick	5	5
Large Roma (plum) tomatoes, cut into 1/2 inch (12 mm) slices	2	2
Olive (or cooking) oil	2 tbsp.	30 mL

Combine first 7 ingredients in large bowl.

Brush next 3 ingredients with olive oil. Preheat barbecue to medium. Place on greased grill. Cook for about 2 minutes per side until grill marks appear. Transfer to cutting board. Let stand until cool enough to handle. Dice tomato. Add to ginger beer mixture. Remove peel from honeydew and cantaloupe wedges. Dice. Add to ginger beer mixture. Stir. Makes about 4 cups (1 L).

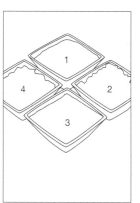

1/4 cup (60 mL): 49 Calories; 1.9 g Total Fat (1.3 g Mono, 0.3 g Poly, 0.3 g Sat); 0 mg Cholesterol; 8 g Carbohydrate; 1 g Fibre; 1 g Protein; 88 mg Sodium

Pictured at left.

1. Chimichurri Aioli, page 139
2. Simple Grilled Salsa, page 150
3. Roasted Red Pepper Sauce, page 135
4. Melon Ginger Salsa, above

Props: Stokes

Texas-Style Mop Sauce

Texas barbecue includes several flavour-building steps: seasoning meat with a rub, smoking over low indirect heat, mopping to retain moisture and serving with a flavourful barbecue sauce for dipping. Use this mop sauce to keep your poultry, pork or beef moist during indirect cooking. It will give the meat gorgeous, rich colour.

Apple cider vinegar	1/2 cup	125 mL
Water	1/4 cup	60 mL
Worcestershire sauce	1/4 cup	60 mL
Chili powder	1 tbsp.	15 mL
Garlic cloves, minced	3	3
(or 3/4 tsp., 4 mL, powder)		
Hot pepper sauce	1 tbsp.	15 mL
Smoked sweet paprika	1 tbsp.	15 mL
Bay leaves	3	3
Medium lemon, halved	1	1

Combine first 8 ingredients in small saucepan. Squeeze lemon juice into saucepan. Add lemon halves. Bring to a boil. Reduce heat to medium-low. Simmer, uncovered, for 15 minutes. Remove and discard lemon halves and bay leaves. Cool. Store in refrigerator in airtight container for up to 1 week. Makes about 1 cup (250 mL).

2 tbsp. (30 mL): 11 Calories; trace Total Fat (0 g Mono, trace Poly, 0 g Sat); trace Cholesterol; 3 g Carbohydrate; trace Fibre; trace Protein; 135 mg Sodium

Tomato Mango Chutney

A smooth sweet-and-sour combination that goes nicely with smoky pork or poultry. With its mild curry flavours, this chutney would also be lovely over rice.

Cooking oil	2 tsp.	10 mL
Chopped onion	1/4 cup	60 mL
Finely grated ginger root	1 tbsp.	15 mL
Ground coriander	1/2 tsp.	2 mL
Ground cumin	1/2 tsp.	2 mL

(continued on next page)

Can of diced tomatoes (with juice)	14 oz.	398 mL
Chopped fresh (or frozen, thawed) mango	1/2 cup	125 mL
Brown sugar, packed	1/4 cup	60 mL
Lime juice	2 tbsp.	30 mL
Salt	1/2 tsp.	2 mL
Pepper	1/4 tsp.	1 mL

Heat cooking oil in medium saucepan on medium. Add next 4 ingredients. Cook for about 5 minutes, stirring often, until onion is softened.

Add remaining 6 ingredients. Stir. Bring to a boil. Reduce heat to medium-low. Simmer, uncovered, for about 45 minutes, stirring occasionally, until thickened. Cool. Store in refrigerator in airtight container for up to 1 week. Makes about 1 1/2 cups (375 mL).

1/4 cup (60 mL): 72 Calories; 1.6 g Total Fat (0.9 g Mono, 0.4 g Poly, 0.1 g Sat); 0 mg Cholesterol; 15 g Carbohydrate; 1 g Fibre; 1 g Protein; 364 mg Sodium

Bacon Blue Cheese Butter

For lovers of butter, bacon and blue cheese. Lovely with steak and potatoes, spread on a burger bun or as a unique twist to "garlic" bread. The prepared butter roll may be frozen for up to 1 month.

Bacon slices, chopped	2	2
Finely chopped onion	1/4 cup	60 mL
Butter, softened	1/4 cup	60 mL
Chopped Stilton cheese	1/4 cup	60 mL

Cook bacon and onion in small frying pan on medium for about 10 minutes until bacon is crisp. Remove with slotted spoon to paper towel-lined plate to drain. Transfer to small bowl.

Add butter and cheese. Beat until combined. Transfer to sheet of waxed paper. Form into 6 inch (15 cm) long log. Wrap in waxed paper. Chill for at least 1 hour until firm. Remove waxed paper. Cut into 1/4 inch (6 mm) slices. Makes about 24 slices.

1 slice: 30 Calories; 3.0 g Total Fat (0.6 g Mono, 0.1 g Poly, 1.9 g Sat); 8 mg Cholesterol; trace Carbohydrate; trace Fibre; 1 g Protein; 48 mg Sodium

Smoky Onion Chutney

A universal condiment great with grilled pork or beef, and excellent spread on a burger bun. For a trip back to merry old England, try serving this with a ploughman's lunch!

Cooking oil	3 tbsp.	50 mL
Chopped onion	4 cups	1 L
Brown sugar, packed	1 tbsp.	15 mL
Smoked sweet paprika	1 tbsp.	15 mL
Salt	1 tsp.	5 mL
Pepper	1/2 tsp.	2 mL
Apple cider vinegar	1/4 cup	60 mL
Brown sugar, packed	1/4 cup	60 mL

Heat cooking oil in large saucepan on medium. Add next 5 ingredients. Cook for about 25 minutes, stirring often, until onion is softened and golden.

Add vinegar and second amount of brown sugar. Stir. Cook for about 5 minutes, stirring occasionally, until liquid is reduced and mixture is thickened. Let stand until cool. Store in refrigerator in airtight container for up to 1 week. Makes about 1 1/4 cups (300 mL).

1/4 cup (60 mL): 179 Calories; 8.5 g Total Fat (4.8 g Mono, 2.5 g Poly, 0.6 g Sat); 0 mg Cholesterol; 27 g Carbohydrate; 2 g Fibre; 1 g Protein; 477 mg Sodium

Kettle Shake Rub

This well-balanced, all-purpose spice mix is loosely based on the flavour theory of salty and sweet that's exemplified by kettle corn. Pairs well with chicken, pork and lamb. As a bonus, you can try it on your popcorn, too!

Granulated sugar	1/4 cup	60 mL
Paprika	1/4 cup	60 mL
Chili powder	1 tbsp.	15 mL
Ground cumin	1 tbsp.	15 mL
Salt	1/2 tsp.	2 mL
Pepper	1 tbsp.	15 mL
Cayenne pepper	1/2 tsp.	2 mL
Ground cloves	1/4 tsp.	1 mL

(continued on next page)

Combine all 8 ingredients in small bowl. Store in airtight container for up to 3 months. Makes about 2/3 cup (150 mL).

1 tbsp. (15 mL): 32 Calories; 0.5 g Total Fat (trace Mono, trace Poly, 0.1 g Sat); 0 mg Cholesterol; 7 g Carbohydrate; 1 g Fibre; 1 g Protein; 119 mg Sodium

Spicy Rhubarb Ketchup

You'll never miss the bottled variety once you try this. Tangy, sweet, spicy and smoky, this ketchup pairs well with chicken and pork. Good as a dipping sauce for sweet potato fries, too.

Chopped fresh (or frozen) rhubarb	3 cups	750 mL
Chopped onion	1 cup	250 mL
Brown sugar, packed	1/2 cup	125 mL
Water	1/2 cup	125 mL
Port wine	1/3 cup	75 mL
Red wine vinegar	1/4 cup	60 mL
Chopped chipotle peppers in adobo sauce (see Tip, page 118)	1 tsp.	5 mL
Salt	1/2 tsp.	2 mL
Mixed pickling spice	1 tbsp.	15 mL
Peel from medium orange, cut into thick strips		

Combine first 8 ingredients in large saucepan. Bring to a boil.

Place pickling spice and orange peel on 10 inch (25 cm) square of cheesecloth. Tie cheesecloth with string to enclose. Submerge in rhubarb mixture. Reduce heat to medium. Cook, uncovered, for about 20 minutes until rhubarb is very soft. Remove and discard cheesecloth bag. Carefully process rhubarb mixture in blender until smooth (see Safety Tip). Let stand until cool. Store in refrigerator in airtight container for up to 1 week. Makes about 1 2/3 cups (400 mL).

2 tbsp. (30 mL): 52 Calories; 0.1 g Total Fat (trace Mono, trace Poly, trace Sat); 0 mg Cholesterol; 11 g Carbohydrate; 1 g Fibre; trace Protein; 94 mg Sodium

Safety Tip: Follow manufacturer's instructions for processing hot liquids.

Simple Grilled Salsa

A quick-to-make condiment to accompany main course chicken, fish or pork chops or appetizer nachos. Jalapeño gives it a spicy kick, and the bold colours will remind you of Mexico. Flavours continue to mellow if chilled overnight.

Olive (or cooking) oil	2 tbsp.	30 mL
Garlic clove, minced	1	1
(or 1/4 tsp., 1 mL, powder)		
Roma (plum) tomatoes, halved lengthwise	6	6
Large jalapeño peppers, halved lengthwise	6	6
Lime juice	1/3 cup	75 mL
Chopped fresh cilantro	1/4 cup	60 mL
Finely chopped red onion	1/4 cup	60 mL
Olive oil	1/4 cup	60 mL
Salt	1/4 tsp.	1 mL
Pepper, sprinkle		

Combine first amount of olive oil and garlic in small cup. Brush 1 tbsp. (15 mL) olive oil mixture over tomato halves. Preheat barbecue to medium-high. Place tomato halves on greased grill. Close lid. Cook for about 3 minutes per side until starting to brown. Let stand until cool enough to handle. Dice. Transfer to medium bowl.

Brush jalapeño peppers with remaining olive oil mixture. Place on greased grill, skin-side down. Close lid. Cook for about 3 minutes until starting to brown. Let stand until cool enough to handle. Remove seeds and ribs (see Tip, below). Chop finely. Add to tomato.

Add remaining 6 ingredients. Stir. Chill, covered, for at least 1 hour to blend flavours. Store in refrigerator in airtight container for up to 3 days. Makes about 3 1/2 cups (875 mL).

1/4 cup (60 mL): 59 Calories; 5.9 g Total Fat (4.2 g Mono, 0.9 g Poly, 0.8 g Sat); 0 mg Cholesterol; 2 g Carbohydrate; 1 g Fibre; trace Protein; 42 mg Sodium

Pictured on page 144.

 tip Hot peppers contain capsaicin in the seeds and ribs. Removing the seeds and ribs will reduce the heat. Wear rubber gloves when handling hot peppers and avoid touching your eyes. Wash your hands well afterwards.

Measurement Tables

Throughout this book measurements are given in Conventional and Metric measure. To compensate for differences between the two measurements due to rounding, a full metric measure is not always used. The cup used is the standard 8 fluid ounce. Temperature is given in degrees Fahrenheit and Celsius. Baking pan measurements are in inches and centimetres as well as quarts and litres. An exact metric conversion is given below as well as the working equivalent (Metric Standard Measure).

Spoons

Conventional Measure	Metric Exact Conversion Millilitre (mL)	Metric Standard Measure Millilitre (mL)
1/8 teaspoon (tsp.)	0.6 mL	0.5 mL
1/4 teaspoon (tsp.)	1.2 mL	1 mL
1/2 teaspoon (tsp.)	2.4 mL	2 mL
1 teaspoon (tsp.)	4.7 mL	5 mL
2 teaspoons (tsp.)	9.4 mL	10 mL
1 tablespoon (tbsp.)	14.2 mL	15 mL

Cups

Conventional Measure	Metric Exact Conversion Millilitre (mL)	Metric Standard Measure Millilitre (mL)
1/4 cup (4 tbsp.)	56.8 mL	60 mL
1/3 cup (5 1/3 tbsp.)	75.6 mL	75 mL
1/2 cup (8 tbsp.)	113.7 mL	125 mL
2/3 cup (10 2/3 tbsp.)	151.2 mL	150 mL
3/4 cup (12 tbsp.)	170.5 mL	175 mL
1 cup (16 tbsp.)	227.3 mL	250 mL
4 1/2 cups	1022.9 mL	1000 mL (1 L)

Dry Measurements

Conventional Measure Ounces (oz.)	Metric Exact Conversion Grams (g)	Metric Standard Measure Grams (g)
1 oz.	28.3 g	28 g
2 oz.	56.7 g	57 g
3 oz.	85.0 g	85 g
4 oz.	113.4 g	125 g
5 oz.	141.7 g	140 g
6 oz.	170.1 g	170 g
7 oz.	198.4 g	200 g
8 oz.	226.8 g	250 g
16 oz.	453.6 g	500 g
32 oz.	907.2 g	1000 g (1 kg)

Oven Temperatures

Fahrenheit (°F)	Celsius (°C)
175°	80°
200°	95°
225°	110°
250°	120°
275°	140°
300°	150°
325°	160°
350°	175°
375°	190°
400°	205°
425°	220°
450°	230°
475°	240°
500°	260°

Pans

Conventional Inches	Metric Centimetres
8x8 inch	20x20 cm
9x9 inch	22x22 cm
9x13 inch	22x33 cm
10x15 inch	25x38 cm
11x17 inch	28x43 cm
8x2 inch round	20x5 cm
9x2 inch round	22x5 cm
10x4 1/2 inch tube	25x11 cm
8x4x3 inch loaf	20x10x7.5 cm
9x5x3 inch loaf	22x12.5x7.5 cm

Casseroles

CANADA & BRITAIN		UNITED STATES	
Standard Size Casserole	Exact Metric Measure	Standard Size Casserole	Exact Metric Measure
1 qt. (5 cups)	1.13 L	1 qt. (4 cups)	900 mL
1 1/2 qts. (7 1/2 cups)	1.69 L	1 1/2 qts. (6 cups)	1.35 L
2 qts. (10 cups)	2.25 L	2 qts. (8 cups)	1.8 L
2 1/2 qts. (12 1/2 cups)	2.81 L	2 1/2 qts. (10 cups)	2.25 L
3 qts. (15 cups)	3.38 L	3 qts. (12 cups)	2.7 L
4 qts. (20 cups)	4.5 L	4 qts. (16 cups)	3.6 L
5 qts. (25 cups)	5.63 L	5 qts. (20 cups)	4.5 L

Recipe Index

153

H

I

J

K

L

M

O

P

155

156

157

Meal Salads

Jean Paré
ORIGINAL SERIES

Kitchen Tested
Company's Coming
Guaranteed Great!™

Meal Salads combines the crispness of fresh produce with the heartiness of grains, pastas, meats and cheeses, and get the best of both worlds—versatile dishes that are simple, fresh, tasty and filling.

Try it

a sample recipe from *Meal Salads*

Russian Wild Rice Salad

Meal Salads, Page 97

Water	1 1/2 cups	375 mL
Salt	1/8 tsp.	0.5 mL
Wild rice	1/2 cup	125 mL
Sour cream	1/3 cup	75 mL
Chopped fresh dill (or 3/4 tsp., 4 mL, dried)	1 tbsp.	15 mL
White wine vinegar	1 tbsp.	15 mL
Dry mustard	1 tsp.	5 mL
Coarsely ground pepper	1/2 tsp.	2 mL
Granulated sugar	1/2 tsp.	2 mL
Hot pepper sauce	1/8 tsp.	0.5 mL
Chopped fresh spinach leaves, lightly packed	2 cups	500 mL
Deli roast beef slices, cut into thin strips	6 oz.	170 g
Diced pickled beets	2/3 cup	150 mL
Diced English cucumber (with peel)	1/2 cup	125 mL
Finely diced pickled onions	1 tbsp.	15 mL

Combine water and salt in small saucepan. Bring to a boil. Add rice. Stir. Reduce heat to medium-low.

Simmer, covered, for about 60 minutes, without stirring, until rice is tender. Drain any remaining liquid. Cool.

Whisk next 7 ingredients in large bowl.

Add remaining 5 ingredients and rice. Toss. Makes about 6 cups (1.5 L).

1 cup (250 mL): 131 Calories; 3.5 g Total Fat (0.1 g Mono, 0.2 g Poly, 1.9 g Sat); 25 mg Cholesterol; 16 g Carbohydrate; 2 g Fibre; 9 g Protein; 286 mg Sodium

Celebrating the Harvest

RECIPES FOR FALL & WINTER GATHERINGS

Whether from the garden, farmers' market or supermarket, harvest ingredients display the bounty and beauty of nature. Entertain a crowd in style, or feed your family comfort food they'll not soon forget—with new delicious recipes that celebrate harvest ingredients. What a lovely way to get through the long fall and winter!